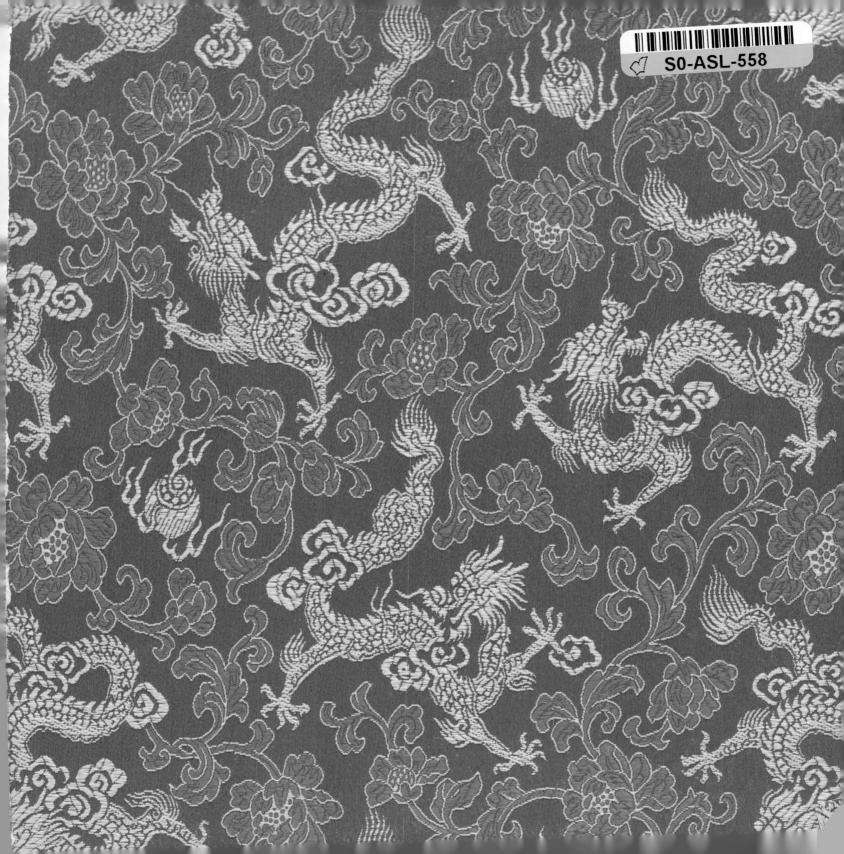

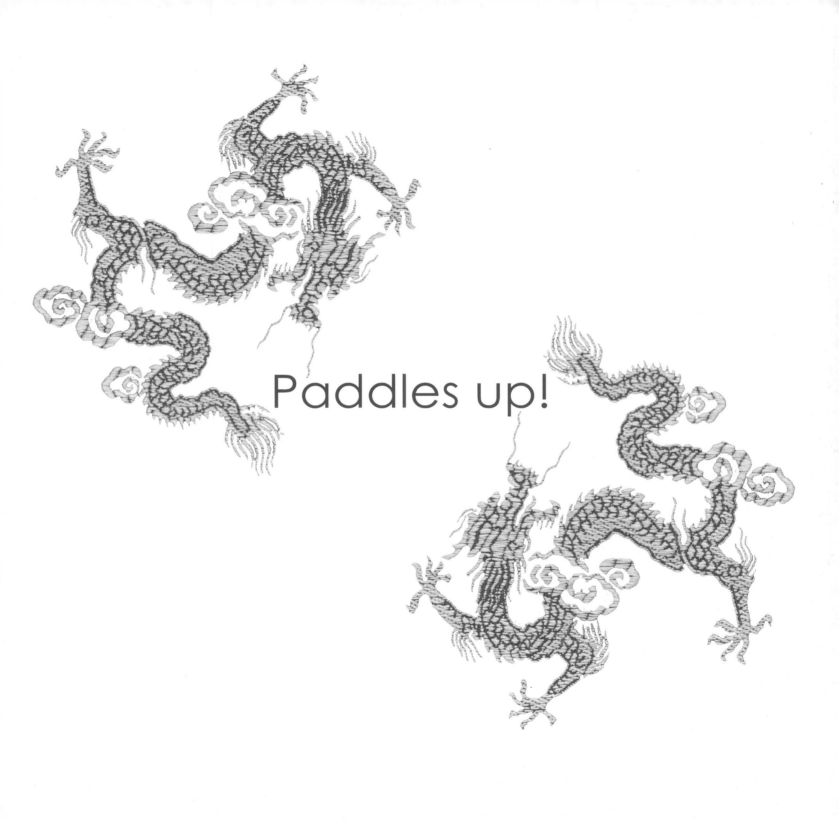

Paddles up!

Paddles up!

Dragon Boat Racing in Canada

Arlene Chan & Susan Humphries

NATURAL HERITAGE BOOKS
DUNDURN PRESS
TORONTO

Editor: Jane Gibson
Copy Editor: Nigel Heseltine
Design: Courtney Horner
Printer: Friesens

Library and Archives Canada Cataloguing in Publication

Chan, Arlene
Paddles up! : dragon boat racing in Canada / by Arlene
Chan and Susan Humphries.

Includes bibliographical references and index.
ISBN 978-1-55488-395-0

1. Dragon boat racing--Canada. 2. Dragon boat
racing. I. Humphries, Susan II. Title.

GV786.C43 2009   797.1'40971   C2009-900295-7

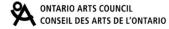

1 2 3 4 5   13 12 11 10 09

We acknowledge the support of the **Canada Council for the Arts** and the **Ontario Arts Council** for our publishing program. We also acknowledge the financial support of the **Government of Canada** through the **Book Publishing Industry Development Program** and **The Association for the Export of Canadian Books**, and the **Government of Ontario** through the **Ontario Book Publishers Tax Credit program**, and the **Ontario Media Development Corporation**.

Front Cover: Copyright © Nicholas Rjabow, iStockphoto.
Top Back Cover: Victoria Dragon Boat Festival in British Columbia. Photograph by William Ng.
Bottom Back Cover: Dragon Beast team from Halifax, Nova Scotia. Photograph by Jan Oakley.

Printed and bound in Canada.
Printed on recycled paper.
www.dundurn.com

Published by Natural Heritage Books
A Member of The Dundurn Group

Dundurn Press	Gazelle Book Services Limited	Dundurn Press
3 Church Street, Suite 500	White Cross Mills	2250 Military Road
Toronto, Ontario, Canada	High Town, Lancaster, England	Tonawanda, NY
M5E 1M2	LA1 4XS	U.S.A. 14150

龙 Contents 船

龙 Foreword 船

DRAGON BOATING: COMMUNITY SPORT FOR ALL, BUT SERIOUS SPORT TOO

≠ ≠

The archaeological record shows that dragon boats were raced in China more than 5,000 years ago. They were used only for ceremonial purposes until the famous poet and statesman Qu Yuan, who lived during China's Warring States Period, was banned from the state of Chu for speaking up against a corrupt regime.

Qu Yuan died some 2,300 years ago by drowning himself in the Miluo River after he learned that the rival state of Qin had defeated his beloved Chu. Qu Yuan's death was commemorated by holding annual dragon boat races. The Dragon Boat Festival evolved from these annual events and eventually spread across China, mainly in the south, and subsequently to other areas in Southeast Asia.

Chinese dragon boat racing is much older than the Ancient Olympic Games held in Greece. In its modern incarnation, it has one major difference from the Greek Olympics. Unlike those games, which celebrated the power and fighting abilities of the warrior class, traditional dragon boat festivals celebrate the sacrifice of Qu Yuan. Ever since his death, racing dragon boats has been a community activity with mass participation to remember his ultimate sacrifice.

The roots of the modern sport of dragon boat racing are also found in southern China and the fishing communities of Hong Kong. "Racing the Dragon" is part of their social life and the skills and traditions of dragon boat racing have been passed on, over hundreds of years, from one generation to the next.

Around the world, there are many other types of traditional long boats, like the dragon boat, which are central to the way of life of local fishing communities. Herein lies the secret and strength of dragon boating. It is truly a sport from the people and for all the people, and one that can bring whole communities together in friendly competition.

Taking part in dragon boating leads to a knowledge of the traditions of the sport. From this knowledge comes an understanding and respect for different cultures and values, and new friendships with people from around the world.

Dragon boat racing in the modern era is also based on participation. It is now a team sport in which people work together to achieve a common goal through common effort. There are no individual "stars" in dragon boat racing. Only the combined efforts of the crew as a whole can bring success and

Having participated in other sports, I have not found one with the social aspects and camaraderie of dragon boating. Even in Malaysia when the races were starting, we would chat with other teams and when we finished racing we would all be congratulating each other for a good race, win or lose.
— Stefan Nowak, Pickering, Ontario

the feeling of complete achievement; individual prowess, unless it can be harnessed for the good of the crew, counts for nought.

But how did this ancient traditional activity develop into today's modern sport? Dragon boating is almost part of daily life in Hong Kong and one of the oldest Chinese traditions. It is not surprising that, in 1975, the Hong Kong Tourist Association (now the Hong Kong Tourist Board) decided that dragon boat racing, with its combination of traditional sporting activity and associated festival of Chinese culture, could be a unique way to promote Hong Kong as a tourist venue.

The first international dragon boat race was then held in Hong Kong in 1976, with a crew from the Japanese city of Nagasaki invited to race. This race launched the modern era of dragon boat racing.

Since then the Hong Kong International Festival Races (HKIR) have taken place annually on the first weekend after the traditional Dragon Boat Festival (Duan Wu Jie) races that are held on the fifth day of the fifth moon, usually in June.

Triggered by the successful marketing campaign that followed, which promoted Hong Kong through the HKIR, dragon boat racing rapidly spread across the world into the Pacific Region, Europe, and North America, but particularly to the United Kingdom and Canada. A tradition of paddling open canoes meant that Canadians took to the dragon boat like the proverbial duck to water!

This explosion of dragon boat activity, emerging out of the Hong Kong International Races, led to the founding of dragon boat associations around the world in the late 1980s. British, Hong Kong, Chinese, and Canadian associations were among the first.

These national organizations, led by the British Dragon Boat Racing Association (BDA), established in 1987, came together and founded the European Dragon Boat Federation (EDBF) in 1990, followed in 1991 by the International Dragon Boat Federation (IDBF), and finally the Asian Dragon Boat Federation (ADBF) in 1992.

Under the guidance of the IDBF the sport has spread to nearly 70 countries on all continents with standard racing rules and regulations formulated by

> In a nutshell, dragon boating is way too much fun to be left out on the dock watching.
> — Lizz Hanan, Victoria, British Columbia

the IDBF. As well, standardized IDBF racing dragon boats and equipment were introduced for world and continental championships in the sport and for adoption by organizations new to the sport.

The modern sport came of age in 2007 when dragon boat racing was recognized as a separate sport from all other paddle sports and the IDBF was admitted into membership of the General Association of International Sports Federations (GAISF) as the international federation and world authority specifically for dragon boating.

Current estimates put the number of participants in dragon boating, worldwide, at over 50 million, of which, it must be said, most are in Southeast Asia. In Hong Kong, for example, around 250,000 paddlers take to the water during the Dragon Boat Festival week. Combined estimates for Europe and North America give a figure of 300,000 people "racing the dragon" each year, of which 70,000 or more are based in Canada.

In Canada, through the efforts of people like Mike Kerkmann from Toronto and his company, Great White North Communications, festival dragon boat racing has developed at an astonishing rate over the past 12 or more years, with community dragon boat races now being held in towns and cities across the country. Recently, it has spread to the United States.

At the international level the IDBF now organizes three levels of world championships: for corporate and community festival racers, for serious dragon boat clubs, and for national dragon boat crews representing their countries at the highest level in the sport.

Heading the list of top nations in dragon boating is Canada, which has won more gold, silver, and bronze medals across the spectrum of championship divisions (premier, junior, and senior) than any other nation, including China, the traditional home of the sport, since the first world championships were held at Yueyang in 1995. Canada also lays claim to having won the Nations Cup for the best Premier Division crew, three times in a row — a feat as yet unmatched by any other nation.

Some 30 years after the first HKIR in 1976, dragon boating has truly become a modern sport for all. The sport has been recognized by the International Olympic Committee (IOC) and has set inclusion in the Olympic Games as its ultimate aim.

A step in the right direction was the inclusion of dragon boat racing in the 2008 Asian Beach Games, and another will be its inaugural participation in the 2010 Asian Games. Meanwhile, by way of a little knock on the IOC's door, 2008 saw the Olympic Flame being carried by dragon boat during both the Hong Kong and Macau legs of the Beijing Olympic Torch relay.

In ending this introduction to the whys and wherefores of dragon boating, may I summarize the whole activity by saying that dragon boat racing is a sport for every level. You can compete with your crew at the highest level of competition, the IDBF World Dragon Boat Racing Championships. You can also compete with your club crew, your colleagues and friends from work, or your local community, and, at each level, enjoy a challenging day of racing.

Dragon boating is technically simple to do and inexpensive to take part in as a healthy activity that can be practised by all ages and ability groups. It is a character-building team sport and, above all, it is GREAT FUN.

See you on the water!

Mike Haslam
Executive President
International Dragon Boat Federation

龙 Introduction 船

Arlene Chan
and
Susan Humphries

We have been fortunate to have paddled and worked with exceptionally dedicated and talented people, not only paddlers and coaches, but also medical and nutritional supporters who all share the same desire to see paddlers realize their full potential and achieve outstanding performances locally, nationally, and on the world stage. They have challenged us.

Whether you are a coach, club member, elite crew hopeful, or simply enjoy a recreational paddle, we hope to challenge you too. Our objectives in assembling this book are to move you closer to the level of paddling to which you aspire and to increase your enjoyment of the sport. You will find many important topics that will expand your knowledge of dragon boating and propel you and your team more efficiently to the finish line.

We have gathered top experts from across the country to explain the world of dragon boating and provide paddling concepts and principles. Mike Haslam was the first to give his enthusiastic support for this book and we give him our deepest thanks. Albert McDonald, national level coach, and elite sprint canoer and paddler, signed on with Suzanne McKenzie, a member of Dragon Beasts and the Canadian Premier Women's Crew, to present the technical elements of the dragon boat stroke. Albert is also the "Voice of the Beast" in chapter 7 that features three postings from *Beast Blog*. Jim Farintosh's stellar

reputation as coach of the Canadian National Crew and Mayfair Predators made him a top choice for penning the chapter on "The Making of an A-Team." Bringing her extensive experience as an Olympian kayaker and dragon boat coach for national teams and the False Creek Racing Canoe Club, Kamini Jain graciously accepted the chapter on coaching. Dr. David Levy, founder of the sports medicine program at McMaster University in Hamilton, contributed the piece on preventing injuries most commonly seen in the sport. As the Strength and Conditioning Director, Athletic Training Professionals, Jamie Hollins — kinesiologist, flatwater paddler, dragon boater, and coach — was a natural choice to cover the topic of dry land training. Eleanor Nielsen brings to life the pioneering work of Dr. Don McKenzie who introduced dragon boating to breast cancer survivors as a therapy that has been embraced by hundreds of teams around the world. Kathy Levy shows how one survivor team has developed into a competitive crew of dedicated paddlers. Pam Collett, with years of experience as a professional coach and national judging official, tackles the topic of nutrition with relish. Mike Kerkmann, who was instrumental in the development of Dragon Boat Canada, is a pioneering service provider, his company, GWN, being the largest in North America. Matt Robert, a former national crew paddler and coach of numerous winning crews, shares his expertise in steering and drumming. Andrew Fox, who is a coach and paddler who has won medals internationally with national crews and the Mayfair Predators, tackles the topic of teams and teamwork. Gerry Kavanagh, as founder of Apex Paddles, represents the new generation of dragon boaters whose entrepreneurial and innovative endeavours have contributed to the sport. And who better than Matt Smith, president of Dragon Boat Canada, could have provided the closing chapter, which tells the story of Canada and its development and prominence on the international scene.

Many thanks are extended to the photographers who graciously granted permission to include their works. Their stunning photographs capture the excitement of our sport and bring words to life with their close-ups of the paddling action from across the country. Thank you to William Ng, Gabe Toth, Laurie Wierzbicki, Fay Wu, Edward Lumb, Albert McDonald, Barry Wojciechowski, VFK, Heather Maclaren, John Valentini, Terry Hewitson, Brent Lessard, Chris Edwards, Normand Beaulieu, Ben Lee, Derek Griffiths, Steven Ercolani, and, particularly, Jan Oakley and Jens Ronneberger. Our gratitude to Kim Ercolani and Suzanne McKenzie for being the fitness and paddling models.

The testimonials that we received were overwhelmingly heartfelt and merit a book of their own.

We could only include a few and thank everyone who took the time to send us their thoughts on what the sport means to them.

The *pinyin* Romanization system, the standard to spell the sounds of Mandarin Chinese, is used throughout this book.

Finally, as paddlers, we remember our first time in a dragon boat, our first coach, our first team, our first race. We all started as beginners. The dragon boat community has given so much to us. We thank all the paddlers, coaches, sponsors, friends, and family to whom we owe so much for the love of dragon boating.

This book is dedicated to our friends and family who have supported our maniacal passion for dragon boating. Richard and Leo, our spouses, deserve our special thanks for their encouragement and understanding … being awakened before sunrise as we fumbled for our paddling gear in the dark to take to the 6:00 a.m. morning practices; putting up with stinky paddling clothes and shoes; spending weeks and weekends alone while we crossed town, province, country, continent, and oceans for race regattas and training camps. We have tested the limits of their tolerance and patience without fail.

Paddles Up!

1

龙 The Beginnings 船

Arlene Chan

Daredevil manoeuvres. Capsized boats. Fierce rivalry. Fighting spectators. So frequent were these incidents that dragon boat races were outlawed in China at the beginning of the twentieth century.[1] The ban was lifted and dragon boating is flourishing as one of the fastest-growing team sports around the world. On the fifth day of the fifth month in the lunar calendar falls the Dragon Boat Festival, one of the most popular Chinese festivals. Celebrated on and off as an unofficial holiday in the People's Republic of China, it became an official state holiday in 2008.

The origins of the dragon boats and the Dragon Boat Festival are buried deep in Chinese history, and many versions abound, all of which share common traditions and rituals, and themes of superstitions, suicides, ghosts, and, most significantly, the dragon.

The Chinese dragon is an ancient mythical creature that has been venerated and honoured as the sacred ruler of the rivers, seas, clouds, and rain. Unlike the fire-breathing and sinister dragon in Western mythology, the Chinese dragon, also known as the River Dragon or Dragon King, was rarely considered malevolent. Although fearsome and powerful, the dragon was worshipped as a benefactor capable of providing enough rainfall for bountiful rice harvests. The dragon's importance throughout Chinese history is evident everywhere — in paintings, literature, sculpture, dance, clothing, architecture, and music. The earliest dragon figure was unearthed in Inner Mongolia on a jar dating back 6,500 years.[2] Later regarded as the official symbol of the emperor during the Yuan dynasty (1279–1368 A.D.), the dragon has come to represent China and its people. But nowhere is the presence of this mythical creature more strongly felt than during the annual Dragon Boat Festival when its heartbeat pulses wildly through millions of dragon boat paddlers around the world.

The story of Qu Yuan is the most popular and recognized account of the origin of the Dragon Boat Festival. Qu Yuan was a respected and well-loved patriot, poet, and statesman who lived during the Warring States Period, a turbulent time in China's history when seven feudal states battled for supremacy. The state of Qin, determined to take over its last major adversary, the state of Chu, offered a truce under the guise of a peace treaty. Qu Yuan advised the king of Chu not to sign any such agreement. Not only did the king sign it but he also banished Qu Yuan for what was perceived as advice from a traitor. Wandering aimlessly and proclaiming his love for the state of Chu, Qu Yuan spent his final years writing what was to become some of China's greatest poetry. When he learned about the fall of Chu to the enemy state of Qin,[3] he clutched a rock to his chest and threw himself into the Miluo River. It was the fifth day of the fifth month in 278 B.C.

When news of his drowning reached the villages, the local fishermen raced out in their boats to try to save their beloved statesman. But it was all to no avail. Beating drums and splashing their paddles on the water, they made every attempt to scare away the fish from eating his body. Dragon boat races are said to re-enact the villagers paddling to Qu Yuan's rescue.

To this day in China, many shrines can be found in his memory. The largest one, Qu Yuan Memorial Hall, was built during the Tang dynasty, and was recently relocated during the construction of the Three Gorges Dam project on the Yangtze River. International dragon boat races have been held annually since 1991 in Qu Yuan's hometown of Yueyang, located in what is known today as Hunan Province.

Less known are other legends associated with the origin of the Dragon Boat Festival, stories that share the theme of individuals whose deaths resulted in cult status like Qu Yuan's. Death by drowning or suicide has been linked to the ancient custom of human sacrifice. Some say that the Dragon Boat Festival is held in honour of a young girl, Cao E. After the drowning of her father, Cao E searched for his body along the riverbank. After many days without any success, she threw herself into the river out of grief and despair. On the fifth day of the fifth month, the bodies of the father and daughter arose together to the water's surface. People were so moved by her filial piety that they commemorate her life and death every year on that day.

Another story, set in the Spring and Autumn period, relates how Wu Zixu, a great military hero and courtier, advised the king of Wu to destroy the defeated state of Yue to prevent a future uprising. Blinded by the veiled obedience of the fallen state, the king did not heed this advice and, instead, ordered Wu Zixu to commit suicide for his dishonourable proposal. On the fifth day of the fifth month, 484 B.C., his body was thrown into the river by order of the king. Ten years later, the state of Yue defeated the state of Wu.

The origin of dragon boats and the Dragon Boat Festival is tied to the rituals and customs associated with an ancient agricultural society, deeply entrenched in ceremonies with dragon-shaped boats well before Qu Yuan's death. The passage of time was marked by the cycles of ploughing the fields, sowing seeds, nurturing the crops, and harvesting. The Dragon Boat Festival, falling on the fifth day of the fifth month, is more accurately represented by its Chinese name, *Duan Wu Jie*, meaning Double Fifth Festival. On this day, the spring season ends and the summer begins. Celebrations honouring this benefactor of rain were held at this time. A contented River Dragon would bring enough rain for prosperous crops. A displeased River Dragon would unleash its wrath by withholding rain and causing droughts, or by

Flag pullers at the Taiwanese Cultural Festival in Vancouver, British Columbia, grab the flags at the finish line. Missing the flag results in disqualification or time penalty.

dispensing too much rain and prompting storms and floods. Capsized boats and drowning during races were considered misfortunes governed by the will of the River Dragon. Casualties were not rescued and those who drowned were considered as sacrifices to venerate the River Dragon. Archaeological excavations show that sacrificial ceremonies were once practised as an important element of many ancient festivals in China. Proof that dragon boating may be the world's oldest, continuing, competitive activity, pre-dating the Olympic Games of ancient Greece by 1,000 years,[4] lies in Hubei Province. There, a drawing of dragon boat races that were depicted on a spinning wheel, 4,000 to 5,000 years old, was excavated from ruins in Qujialing.[5]

Historical records show the existence of dragon boats outside of China in Cambodia and Vietnam in the third century A.D., and also in Japan, Borneo, Thailand, and Burma. Taiwan started holding dragon boat races in 1736 and developed them

The *yin yang* symbol represents an ancient Chinese understanding of how the *yin* and *yang* energies are mutually arising, interdependent, and continuously transforming one into the other. It is also a depiction of the celestial phenomenon of the cycle of the sun, four seasons, and the Chinese calendar.

into major sporting events. A popular and unique feature of the Taiwan dragon boat race crews is the flag puller or flag catcher who is positioned at the front of the dragon boat. Nearing the end of the race, this person assumes the critical task of leaning over the dragonhead and pulling the flag positioned at the finish line of the race lane. The first flag puller to grab the flag wins the race for the team.

TRADITIONS AND CUSTOMS OF THE DRAGON BOAT FESTIVAL

⹌ ⹌

The fifth day of the fifth month was considered the most evil and poisonous day of the year, the beginning of the summer when disease, illness, and death were rampant. Many traditions developed to harmonize the two opposing but complementary forces of *yin* and *yang* that were most strongly unbalanced at the onset of the summer. Without the harmony of these dual forces that permeated all life and the universe, the powers of nature wreaked havoc. The symbol of *yin yang* evokes the harmonious interplay of opposites.

Precautions were taken against the presiding evils of the season, a time for preventive activities in old China. The "Five Poisons" that were prevalent in the fifth month were represented by the snake, lizard, toad, centipede, and scorpion. These poisonous and harmful creatures contributed to calamities and the spread of diseases. To combat these evils, their images were prominently incorporated on clothing, cakes, and lucky charms with the belief that the accumulated effect of these five poisons would successfully combat all other ones. The lucky charms, in the form of "fragrant pouches" or *xiangbao*, were filled with aromatic herbs and worn by children as protection. Five-coloured threads were given as gifts to avert evil. The five elements of wood, fire, earth, metal, and water were repre-

Fragrant pouches are made with cotton or silk and filled with aromatic herbs to prevent illness. These are given to children during the Dragon Boat Festival.

Photograph by Edward Lumb

Photograph by Barry Wojciechowski

Dotting the eye of the dragon is the ceremonial rite that brings life to the dragon boat and ends its slumber in storage. A local dignitary in Thunder Bay, Ontario, is given this honorary task.

sented by the five colours of azure, red, yellow, white, and black, all working in harmony to banish bad luck. Another defence against evil was the fierce-looking ghost of Zhong Kui always shown brandishing his sword. His portrait was prominently displayed in homes during the festival to guard families from evil ghosts and demons. Branches of calamus, mugwort, and moxa were also hung around the home to ward off misfortune and prevent disease. Many of these precautionary measures remain popular today during the Dragon Boat Festival.

An ancient ritual that continues to be practised, though without its deep religious roots, is the "awakening of the dragon" after the long sleep in storage. Typically, a Daoist priest conducts the ceremony with chanting to ward off evil spirits. Blessing the boats and the burning of paper money and incense makes the boats strong and fierce for the races to follow. The traditional "dotting the eye" ceremony in modern times involves community dignitaries awakening the dragon by dabbing red paint on the dragon's eye. Red is the colour that symbolizes heat, summer, and fire and represents good fortune and prosperity.

When we get out on the water, I leave it all on the dock, secure in the knowledge that I am surrounded by a strong group of like-minded women who share the same issues, who care deeply about each other and who will work their hardest to reach a common goal ...
— Nancy Jones, Toronto

Women were not allowed in dragon boats until modern times. Rather, they paddled in phoenix boats.[6] In Chinese mythology, the dragon exemplified the masculine principle of *yang* and the phoenix, the feminine principle of *yin* in the Chinese ideology of cosmic harmony. Both the sun and the dragon are considered to be male (*yang*) forces and are most powerful at this time of the year.[7] Once the dragon was awakened in the ceremony, it had to be treated with respect and protected from anything that might diminish its *yang* character, such as contact with women. As a result, dragon boat racing was a ritual celebration that excluded women.

Of all the customs associated with the Dragon Boat Festival, none rival that of the preparation and eating of *zongzi*, sticky rice dumplings wrapped in leaves. The story behind these rice delicacies is linked to Qu Yuan. After the villagers arrived too late in their boats to save Qu Yuan from drowning, some say that they threw rice into the water, which the fish or the River Dragon, by other accounts, would eat instead of Qu Yuan's body. Others say that the rice was to feed the spirit of Qu Yuan in his afterlife. While the real reason remains obscured, the custom of eating *zongzi* has endured until today. *Zongzi* can be purchased year-round at Chinese restaurants, stores, and bakeries. And, Chinese families continue making these delicacies during the Dragon Boat Festival, their own special recipes handed down through generations.

Photograph by Edward Lumb

Zongzi from Beijing are filled with sweet ingredients, like bean paste, walnuts, and dates. In southern China, they are made with salty fillings, like roast duck, chicken, peanuts or salted duck eggs. The third type is preserved in a strong alkaline solution.

We wear kilts and have lucky Chinese coins on our team jersey. We eat Asian foods and Scottish haggis — sometimes combined. It's become more than just being social.... It's become a family.
— Todd Wong, Vancouver, British Columbia

Dragon boat races, rooted in the ancient past of gods, ghosts, and superstitions, treaded unfamiliar waters in Western communities for thousands of years. Only recently have they become sporting events that promise fanfare, drums, and excitement. Traditions and rituals are re-enacted in ceremonies to awaken and dot the eye of the dragon, and in dragon boat racing itself. The Dragon Boat Festival, the most international of all festivals from China, is the only one embraced by Chinese and non-Chinese alike. The lure of dragon boating arouses deep passion in the hearts of men and women, young and old.

NOTES

1. Carol Stephanchuk and Charles Wong, *Mooncakes and Hungry Ghosts: Festivals of China* (San Francisco: China Books, 1992).
2. Bian Yi, *China Daily*, November 29, 1999.
3. With the fall of the last independent state of Chu, the Qin kingdom unified all other states into the first Chinese empire to be ruled by Qin Shi Huang, the first emperor of China. The English word for *China* is considered to be derived from *Qin* (pronounced "Cheen").
4. *International Dragon Boat Federation Handbook*, 4th edition (IDBF, 2004).
5. *Ibid*.
6. Henning Wiekhorst, *Hong Kong: Mother of Dragons* (Hong Kong: Creative-Dragon-Works, 2006).
7. Another translation of "Duan Wu" is "maximum sun" or "upright sun." On the fifth day of the fifth month, the male forces (*yang*) are at maximum intensity and the sun reaches it highest position in the sky.

Sources

Barker, Pat. *Dragon Boats: A Celebration*. Vancouver: Raincoast Books, 1996.

Bodde, Derk. *Festivals in Classical China*. Princeton, NJ: Princeton University Press, 1975.

Chan, Arlene. *Awakening the Dragon: The Dragon Boat Festival*. Toronto: Tundra Books, 2004.

Eberhard, Wolfram. *Chinese Festivals*. New York: Abelard-Schuman, 1958.

Huxley, Francis. *The Dragon: Nature of Spirit, Spirit of Nature*. London: Thames and Hudson, 1989.

Jones, Meg. *Chinese New Year and the Dragon Boat Festival*. London: Scholastic, 2004.

Law, Joan, and Barbara Ward. *Chinese Festivals in Hong Kong*. Hong Kong: *South China Morning Post*, 1982.

Vasu, Suchitthra. *Dragon Boat Festival*. Singapore: National Library of Singapore, 1997.

Stepanchuk, Carol. *Red Eggs and Dragon Boats*. Berkeley, CA: Pacific View Press, 1994.

Stepanchuk, Carol, and Charles Wong. *Mooncakes and Hungry Ghosts: Festivals in China*. San Francisco: China Books, 1992.

Wiekhorst, Henning. *Hong Kong: Mother of Dragons*. Hong Kong: Creative-Dragon-Works, 2006.

2

龙 船

Basic Dragon Boat Paddling Technique

Albert McDonald
and
Suzanne McKenzie

Efficient paddling technique, which engages the body's core muscle groups, promotes the following: first, maximum "glide" or boat run; second, reduced stress on smaller muscle groups, thereby reducing the chance of sport injury; third, the burning of more calories by engaging and utilizing large, versus small, muscle groups; fourth, the contribution to increased boat speed.

Though some crews may not be interested in boat speed, most crews are. Often, coaches will offer increased boat speed as the sole reason to make technical changes and to paddle efficiently; however, boat speed is not the sole reason to paddle efficiently.

Several key elements of the proper paddling technique are listed and described below. Many different styles and perspectives on technique are prevalent. In general, style refers to sequencing of body movements and movement of the paddle when the paddle is out of the water. Dragon boat attracts many experienced, world-class paddlers from other paddling disciplines, such as flatwater, marathon, outrigger, et cetera. These paddlers have developed different stroke aspects, even bad habits, but can maintain extremely powerful connection with the water. Their high fitness level, built over many years and combined with their water connection, enables them to paddle extremely effectively in dragon boat. Through a different "style" they are still able to achieve boat efficiency — when the paddle

is in the water, the blade angle is optimal and they are engaging core muscles. Therefore, there are different ways to be successful and achieve boat efficiency, particularly when the paddle is out of the water.

Dragon Boat Stroke for Basic Beginner to Mid-Competitive Level Paddlers
≠ ≯

Establishing stability and proper positioning in the boat is the key to transferring power to the water to create boat glide and therefore speed.

Basic Preparation

Before describing the elements of the proper stroke technique, we will outline the proper base of support (seated position in the dragon boat) and how to choose a paddle and hold the paddle correctly. *If you do not have a proper base of support or if you hold the paddle incorrectly, you will not be able to achieve an efficient technique.*

Base of Support

The seated position involves correct placement of the feet and the buttocks.

When getting into the boat, paddlers should sit as close as possible to the gunwale on the side they are paddling so that the hips are snug to each paddler's side of the boat (see Figure 1).

The outside leg, that is, the leg closest to the gunwale, from hip to knee, will touch the side of the boat — depending on the person's position in the boat. It is easier to get more of your leg against the side in the very front of the boat.

The feet need to be positioned firmly on the foot

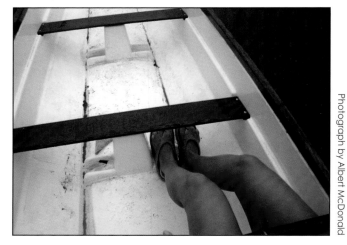

Figure 2: Heels on Rib.

hold, called a rib, in front of the paddlers and underneath the seat in front of them. In the dragon boat, there is a double rib in front of each paddler. Depending on the height of the paddler, the first rib or the one ahead of it will be used. It is important that paddlers position their feet so that they can push firmly with the feet at the beginning, or top, of each stroke. The push with the feet works in conjunction with the pull phase of the stroke to propel the boat forward and create power and boat speed (see Figure 2).

Note: Some paddlers push with two feet and some tuck the inside leg back. The most important

Figure 1: Hip and Leg.

factor is that the paddler can push solidly and create sufficient resistance.

Remember: The most important factors with respect to establishing a solid base of support in a dragon boat are: First, that three points of contact — pulling side hip, buttocks, and feet — are in a solid, static position as far away from the centre of the boat as possible, and second, that the body weight is distributed over these three points of contact and the paddler is not "sitting" in the boat.

Holding the Paddle

There are three parts to the paddle: the top of the paddle that is often shaped like a "T" and, therefore, called the T-grip; the shaft or middle part of the paddle; and the blade of the paddle, of which the bottom, wider portion goes in the water.

The top hand holds the T-grip with a comfortable grip (see Figure 3). There is no need to hold it too tightly or the paddler may get hand cramps. The bottom hand grips the shaft of the paddle a half of a fist, approximately one inch, above the blade portion of the paddle. The bottom hand should not be directly on top of the blade as there must be space

between the top of the blade and the bottom hand (see Figure 4). The most effective point to create force with a paddle is at the direct midpoint as measured from the paddle tip to the top of the T-grip. Marking this point with a piece of tape can help, particularly for beginners. Tape can also be used to prevent the bottom hand slipping or sliding up the shaft of the paddle. Some people who are concerned about this movement wear gloves but most world-level paddlers believe that gloves restrict the ability to "feel" the water and only wear gloves in very cold water conditions.

Photographs by Albert McDonald

Figure 3 (left): Top Hand Position.
Figure 4 (right): Bottom Hand Position.

Choosing a Paddle

The basic size for dragon boat paddles is 116 centimetres (46 inches). As individuals commit to the sport, they will likely want to invest in a personal paddle. When choosing to purchase a paddle, they will consider whether they want a wooden paddle, a fibreglass paddle, or a lighter, more durable paddle made of carbon fibre. Most high-performance paddlers choose the lighter carbon-fibre paddles; however, these are more expensive. Individuals also need to consider correct paddle size as the standard length is not appropriate for many paddlers.

To determine the proper dragon boat paddle size, turn the paddle upside down while seated in the boat (see Figure 5). The T-grip portion of the paddle should be closest to the water. With the bottom hand holding the paddle one hand length from the blade, extend the bottom arm to the forward "catch" position, as shown in Figure 5. The top of the T-grip should barely touch the water. Paddlers should try this before ordering their paddles to help determine a proper size because some paddles, once ordered, cannot be made any longer. Some people who move around to different positions in the boat purchase adjustable paddles. Differences in paddle size requirements depend on the position you are in the boat. In the front of the

Photograph by Albert McDonald

Figure 5: Extension Position.

boat, in particular, a paddler needs a shorter paddle because of the bow wave.

1. Top (Front) of the Stroke

≠ ≭

Core/Hip Rotation

This part of the technique helps paddlers achieve maximum reach and extends the length of the stroke. Longer strokes generally increase boat speed.

Rotation is started as the outside (pulling side) hip pushes forward toward the front of the boat and the gunwale side leg is pushed forward by the hip motion. The hip on the inside of the boat (closest to middle of the boat) will, at the same time, move slightly back. This movement causes the core/midsections of paddlers to rotate forward so that their backs turn on an angle toward the gunwale (see Figure 6).

Next, the gunwale side shoulder turns forwards and the top arm shoulder moves backward (see Figure 7).

The head and neck must remain facing forward and must not rotate with the body.

Figure 7: Early Rotation.

Figure 6: Hips Rotating.

Figure 8: Full Rotation.

Photograph by Albert McDonald

35

At full rotation, the paddler's back is angled facing the gunwale side of the boat while the midsection and stomach are angled to face the middle of the boat. As much as possible, the shoulders are "stacked" with the top shoulder over the bottom shoulder (see Figure 8).

Arm Extension

To complete the front part of the stroke, the paddler must extend the arms. Most beginners will keep their hands too close to their bodies, particularly the top hand. As paddlers rotate their hips, torso, and

Photograph by Albert McDonald

Figure 9: Arms at Full Extension.

shoulders, they should extend both arms completely, to reach up the side of the boat, and lean forward slightly (see Figure 9).

When fully extended and rotated, a paddler should essentially be able to see the outside of the boat. The body should be extended as far as possible on the outside of the boat. The body weight at this point is on the outside of the boat getting ready to come down onto the paddle with full force as it enters the water.

Paddle Position

The paddle, at this point (full extension and rotation), which is called the top or front of the stroke, should be vertical, at a positive angle to the water (see Figure 9) and as close to the side of the boat as possible without hitting it. The paddler should try to keep this vertical paddle position, as much as possible, throughout the entire stroke to the exit phase.

Remember: Apply force as close to the midpoint of the boat as possible. Keep your body weight as far from the midpoint of the boat as possible.

2. CATCH PHASE

≠ ≠

Catch

The catch of the stroke is the point at which the paddle enters the water at the top of the stroke. An effective and focused catch is essential. The top hand should push downwards on the grip of the paddle to drive the paddle into the water and place the full body weight of the paddler onto the blade. Generally called the transfer of power, this is the point of the stroke where paddlers must use their body weight and top arm strength together to create the initial force as their paddles enter the water. The paddle should enter the water at the most positive angle possible, assuming correct top arm position that is square to the side of the boat (see Figure 10).

Remember: Top arm position is critical to having an effective and powerful catch.

Connection

At this moment, paddlers should feel the weight of the water on their paddles. They need to maximize the resistance that is felt on their blades as they enter the water. A strong connection with the water is what makes the boat go fast. Ideally, paddlers should feel the same "weight of the water" on their paddles throughout the entire pull phase of the stroke.

Connection is the most important factor to make the boat go fast. When someone says that certain paddlers have real connection with the water or that they are pulling hard, the comment means that these paddlers have transferred their body weight to the paddle and created resistance between the paddle

Photograph by Albert McDonald

Figure 10: Catch and Entry.

Photograph by Albert McDonald

Figure 11: Paddle at Vertical Position.

and the water. Often you can see the water coming off the back of the paddle at the end of the stroke in small, tornado-like movements, if a paddler has good connection with the water. Good paddlers will not throw water or "shovel" water on the exit because this is a sign that they are losing resistance during the back half of the stroke (see Figure 11).

Remember: The paddler creates resistance on the blade with the water and pulls the boat up to the paddle, not the paddle to the boat.

3. PULL PHASE (FOOT PUSH)

≠ ≒

The catch begins the pull phase of the actual stroke. The *front half* of the stroke is the pulling phase from the catch to about the knee.

At this point, the body begins to unwind or counter rotate, keeping the arms as straight as possible, while pulling the water back with the big muscles in the back and the midsection or core of the body. If the paddler is rotated at the catch, the counter rotation occurs simply by sitting up and keeping constant pressure with the top arm.

The top arm pushes down on the paddle while the bottom arm acts as a guide moving with the body and pulling back at the same time. When the bottom hand pulls back, it keeps the top hand from driving the paddle too deep. The blade should be buried completely in the water but the bottom hand should not enter the water. The *counter rotation* is what actually moves the boat forward, not the bottom arm.

At the same time, the paddler pushes with the feet to get more connection with the water and to create more resistance. Constant pressure on your heels against the rib is important as you sit up. This movement allows you to press your hips forward and "slide" the boat. For beginners, this is a difficult skill, but if they use foot pressure at an early stage they will develop this skill with more experience. At a beginner level, paddlers need to sit up tall and not "collapse" forward.

The paddle position remains vertical and close to the side of the boat throughout the entire stroke. This is important if the paddler wants to avoid scooping the water, like you would shovel dirt or snow, resulting in downward, not forward, boat run.

At the *back half* of the stroke, the paddler wants to focus on maintaining the push with the feet and the connection with the water while sitting up hard just as the paddle comes out of the water. It is important to maintain top arm pressure while sitting up.

Remember: Press down while sitting up. Try to connect your stomach by pressing with your feet. You are pulling your body to the paddle, not the paddle to your body.

4. Exit and Recovery

$$\neq \; \rlap{\,/}{\uparrow}$$

At the end of the stroke, the paddle must exit the water cleanly. The paddler should be sitting up at the end of the stroke (see Figure 12).

Begin the exit mid-thigh and do not bring the paddle back past your seat or buttocks.

The top and the bottom arms pull the paddle out of the water. The top hand should remain in front of the paddler's face as much as possible and should be over the side of the boat. It will swing in a small circle

Photograph by Albert McDonald

Figure 12: Exit Position.

Figure 13: Exit Position.

coming momentarily inside the boat when the paddle exits the water (see Figure 13).

This begins the recovery phase that sets up the body and the paddle again to take the next stroke. The paddler should quickly snap the paddle to the front of the stroke using the same rotation and arm extension described at the beginning of this section. The paddler should be as relaxed as possible on the recovery (see Figure 14).

Remember: Do not exit past the hip. Relax and breathe (inhale) on the recovery. Stretch forward. Give yourself time to rotate. Slow down the recovery, particularly if you are a beginner. Trust a longer, more efficient stroke.

Timing

Timing is the most important aspect of generating boat speed. All 20 paddlers must paddle in unison to create optimum boat run. Paddlers, on the left and right sides, and from the front to the back of the boat, need to put their paddles in the water simultaneously and exit simultaneously. For timing to be effective, there are four important elements:

- First, the paddles must enter the water at the same time and at the same speed. Paddlers can look up the boat at the paddle in front of them, they can use the movement of the person beside

Figure 14: Initiating Recovery.

them, and they can use the sound or rhythm of the water and the paddles connecting.

- Second, the catch and pull phases need to happen at the same time. Matching the torso movements of the paddler in front helps to check this.
- Third, paddles should all exit the water together. This is probably the most important aspect of timing and boat run.
- Fourth, the torso, hip, leg, and paddle movements on the recovery occur together.

Remember: There are many cues to use to help with timing. Ultimately, paddlers will be able to use only the feel of the boat to stay in rhythm. Exercises, such as "20 strokes eyes closed, 20 strokes eyes open," help to achieve this feel.

Stroke Rate and Power

Each crew must find its optimal stroke rate, the speed at which each stroke occurs. This rate will differ slightly from crew to crew. Some world class crews have very fast stroke rates while others have slower ones. Essentially, the key is finding the rate where all paddlers can get full rotation and power each time the paddle enters the water. If the rate is too fast then the power can suffer and boat speed will decline. If the rate is too slow then boat speed can also suffer. The rate will change based on the length of a race or timed piece. Shorter distances and times will generally be more sprint-like and have a faster pace because paddlers only have to maintain the fast rate for a short distance and maintain the power for a shorter period of time. Longer pieces generally have longer and slower stroke rates so that the force on the paddle can be maintained equally throughout the race. Stroke rate is a factor of the following: fitness and skill level; size of the athletes; and strength of the athletes.

Remember: The rate is generally dictated by the paddlers who sit in the middle of the boat and usually have the longest range of motion and power transmission. The people in the front and back of the boat need to take the extra time that they have to ensure maximum rotation during the recovery phase of the stroke.

SUMMARY

≠ ≠

Always start with the basics — position in the boat, correct paddle grip and size, hand position at paddle entry and exit, breathing (inhale on recovery), and rotation and timing.

Relax on the recovery (when you are not moving the boat) and relax the non-pulling muscles (face, neck, wrists, hands).

Try to paddle on both sides to prevent injury and to correct bad habits.

Use your core muscle groups. Engage in off-water activities that exercise the core and promote dynamic movement, particularly in the winter.

Practise long pulling and always try for boat run.

Have fun!

3

龙 Getting There: 船
Dry Land Training

Jamie Hollins

What a great exercise and mother-daughter-time sport. We both are muscle girls and this sport is toning our bodies like no other sport I have done. The competition is fierce and the rewards are worth all the hard work.
— Michelle Thiessen, Chilliwack, British Columbia

Getting there? How do you prepare for a dragon boat season? First, you must look at the specific requirements of dragon boat paddling. Then you break down each of them so you can train properly in the gym and use other cross-training modalities that will assist your goal of becoming the best you can be come race day. Dragon boating is a unique sport. It requires all energy systems: ATP-CP and LA; LA-O2; and O2. Combined with these energy system requirements, success in dragon boating demands maximum strength, power, muscular endurance, core flexibility/stability, and power endurance. To prepare correctly, you must understand what you are trying to accomplish so that you can plan, that is, periodize, your training accordingly. Having knowledge about the energy systems that you are training and looking at the most efficient way to train them to accomplish strength gains in all areas is important. As well, proper warm-up, cool-down, and dry land options are crucial to dragon boating.

Energy production is both time- and intensity-related. Paddling at a high intensity, as in a start or sprint, means that an athlete cannot operate effectively for long. Paddling at a low intensity, as in gentle paddling, means that an athlete can sustain activity for extended periods. Training introduces another variable; the 200-metre specialist who uses sound training principles will be able to paddle at a high intensity for longer periods. Similarly, the 2,000-metre dragon boat specialist who uses sound training methods can sustain higher intensities during a set period. The goal is to create the all-round dragon boater who can be effective at all events — 200, 500, 1,000, and 2,000 metres.

ENERGY PATHWAYS

In their book *The Physiological Basis of Physical Education and Athletics*,[1] the authors, Matthews and Fox, divide the running requirements of various sports into the following energy pathways: ATP-CP and LA; LA-O2; and O2, all of which can be directly related to dragon boating.

ATP

Adenosine triphosphate (ATP) is a complex chemical compound that is formed with the energy released from food and stored in all cells, particularly muscles. Cells can perform work only from the energy released by the breakdown of ATP and it is this breakdown that produces energy and adenosine diphosphate (ADP).

CP

Creatine phosphate (CP) is a chemical compound stored in muscle. When it beaks down, CP aids in the manufacture of ATP. The combination of ADP and CP produces ATP.

LA

Lactic acid (LA) is a fatiguing metabolite of the lactic acid system. It results from the incomplete breakdown of glucose. Although excessive lactate production is part of the extreme fatigue process, the protons that are simultaneously produced further restrict performance.

O2

The energy pathway of O2 is the source for aerobic paddling when ATP is manufactured from food sources, mainly sugar and fat. This system produces ATP copiously and acts as the primary energy source during endurance activities.

Running Duration Compared to Dragon Boating

Duration	Dragon Boating	Classification	Energy Supplied By
1 to 4 seconds	5 strokes	Anaerobic	ATP (in muscles)
4 to 10 seconds	Start	Anaerobic	ATP + CP
10 to 45 seconds	Start to 200 m	Anaerobic	ATP + CP + Muscle glycogen
45 to 120 seconds	Transition to 500 m	Anaerobic, Lactic	Muscle glycogen
120 to 240 seconds	500 to 1000 m	Aerobic + Anaerobic	Muscle glycogen + lactic acid
240 to 600 seconds	1000 to 2000 m	Aerobic	Muscle glycogen + fatty acids

All these energy pathways have time limits. A specific pathway is no longer used once a certain time elapses. Although there is some controversy about these limitations, the preceding chart relates the running duration with the approximated race components of dragon boating to show the use of the energy systems.

Muscle contraction produces ADP that is regenerated when coupled with CP. When muscles are actively contracted, they obtain ATP from the glucose that is stored in the bloodstream and from the breakdown of glycogen that is stored in the muscles. For exercise that lasts for longer periods, the complete oxidation of carbohydrates or free fatty acids in the mitochondria is required. The carbohydrate supply lasts approximately 90 minutes and the free fatty store lasts several days.

At the start of exercise, all three energy systems are actively contributing. The contribution, however, depends on the individual, the effort applied, and the rate at which energy is used. The following graph shows how the energy systems contribute to the manufacture of ATP over time when exercise is at 100 percent effort. The thresholds (T) indicate the point at which the energy system is exhausted. Training will improve the threshold times.

Because dragon boat paddling is one-sided and upper-body dominant, energy system training that simulates the motion of the stroke as much as possible is highly recommended. To properly and specifically train the energy systems for dragon boating, the suggested dry land training apparatus is the Multistroke, the first ergometer specifically designed for dragon boat athletes. Unlike any other ergometer, Multistroke replicates the catch, resistance and glide to give the on-the-water feel of dragon boat paddling. The

Energy Systems and Production of ATP

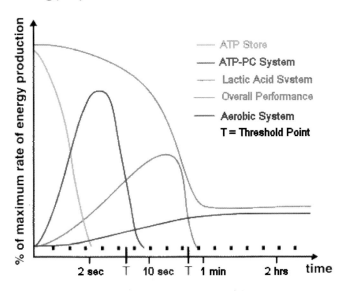

Graph adapted from Brian Mackenzie's Energy Pathways.
http://www.brianmac.co.uk/energy.htm

Courtesy of KayakPro

The Multistroke Ergometer replicates in-the-boat paddling action for dry land training with computer monitoring of distance, time, stroke rate, heart rate, and speed.

Courtesy of Concept2

The erg is a rowing machine that consists of a handle affixed by cable to a flywheel. A counter ticks off the revolutions of the flywheel, a timer paces the rower, and an adjustable brake can be set for body weight and the level of work.

Running Distances Compared to Paddling Times

Running Distance (metres)	Approximate Paddling Time (seconds)
20	2-4
40	5-7
60	7-11
100	11-20
200	21-40
400	60-90
800	120-210
1000	210-360
1200	360-480

mechanics of blade entry and the relationship between the forces on the shaft and the top guiding hand all are replicated. If a Multistroke is unavailable, a rowing ergometer, commonly called the "erg," is the next best alternative for dry land training.

If you have access to an OC-1 or OC-6, paddling on an outrigger is the best way to simulate a dragon boat stroke on the water — highly recommended for specific system training.

If these options are not available, running is another way to train effectively. The training distances outlined above relate running distances to paddling times.

Photograph by Brent Lessard

Many dragon boaters find that paddling in small boats, like the OC-1, is the most effective way to improve water feel and connection.

ANAEROBIC (ATP-CP) ENERGY SYSTEM

≠ ⧧

The supply of ATP in the muscle lasts for approximately two seconds and the re-synthesis of ATP from CP will continue until the CP stores are depleted in about four to six seconds. Approximately five to eight seconds of ATP production is available.

To develop this energy system, sessions of four to eight seconds of high-intensity work at near peak velocity are required, for example:

- 3×(10×30 metres) with recovery of 30 seconds/repetition and five minutes/set;
- 15×60 metres with 60 seconds recovery;
- 20×20 metres shuttle runs with 45 seconds recovery. A shuttle run consists of continuous running between two lines.

ANAEROBIC LACTATE (GLYCOLYTIC) SYSTEM

≠ ⱦ

The body resorts to stored glucose for ATP when the CP supply is depleted. In anaerobic conditions, the breakdown of glucose or glycogen results in the production of lactate and hydrogen ions. The accumulation of hydrogen ions is the limiting factor that causes fatigue in runs of 300 metres to 800 metres. Sessions to develop this energy system are outlined below:

- 5 to 8×300 metres fast — 45 seconds recovery — until pace significantly slows;
- 150-metre intervals at 400 metres pace — 20 seconds recovery — until pace significantly slows;
- 8×300 metres — three minutes recovery (lactate recovery training).

Within the anaerobic lactate system, there are three different working units: Speed Endurance; Special Endurance 1; and Special Endurance 2. Each of these can be developed, as follows:

Working Units of Anaerobic Lactate System

	Speed Endurance	Special Endurance 1	Special Endurance 2
Intensity	95 to 100%	90 to 100%	90 to 100%
Distance	80 to 150 m	150 to 300 m	300 to 600 m
No of Repetitions/Set	2 to 5	1 to 5	1 to 4
No of Sets	2 to 3	1	1
Total distance/session	300 to 1200 m	300 to 1200 m	300 to 1200 m
Example	3 × (60, 80, 100)	2 × 150 m + 2 × 200 m	3 × 500 m

Aerobic Energy System

$$\neq \not=$$

Proteins, fat, and carbohydrate (glycogen) are used by the aerobic energy system to re-synthesize ATP. To develop this energy system, various intensity (tempo) runs can be done, such as the types of tempo runs described below:

Continuous Tempo: Long slow runs at 50 to 70 percent of maximum heart rate place demands on muscle and liver glycogen. The energy system responds by enhancing the capacity of muscle and liver glycogen storage and glycolytic activity associated with these processes.

Extensive Tempo: Continuous runs at 60 to 80 percent of maximum heart rate place demands on the system to cope with lactate production. Running at this tempo assists the removal and turnover of lactate and enhances the body's ability to tolerate greater levels of lactate.

> I thoroughly enjoy the mental and physical challenges of training. Racing is a rush and competitive success is pure joy. However, it's sharing these moments — the many highs and lows of training and competition — with 22 teammates-turned-friends that makes dragon boat more gratifying than anything I've previously experienced in sport.
> — Andrew Simpson, Toronto

Intensive Tempo: Continuous runs at 80 to 90 percent of maximum heart rate result in high lactate levels as these runs border on speed endurance and special endurance. Intensive tempo training lays the base for the development of anaerobic energy systems.

Sessions to develop this energy system are:

- 4 to 6×2 to 5 minute runs — 2 to 5 minutes recovery
- 20×200 metres — 30 seconds recovery
- 10×400 metres — 60 to 90 seconds recovery
- 5- to 10-kilometre runs

ENERGY SYSTEM RECRUITMENT

≠ ≒

All energy systems turn on at the same time and the recruitment of an alternative system occurs when

Contribution of Energy Pathways In Sports

Sport	ATP-CP and LA (%)	LA-O2 (%)	O2 (%)
Dragon boating	30	50	20
Basketball	60	20	20
Fencing	90	10	0
Field events	90	10	0
Golf swing	95	5	0
Gymnastics	80	15	5
Hockey	50	20	30
Distance running	10	20	70
Rowing	20	30	50
Skiing	33	33	33
Soccer	50	20	30
Sprints	90	10	0
Swimming 1.5 km	10	20	70
Tennis	70	20	10
Volleyball	80	5	15

Table adapted from Fox E. L. et al,
The Physiological Basis for Exercise and Sport, 1993

the current energy system is almost depleted. Given that most dragon boaters compete at all events — 200 metres, 500 metres, 1,000 metres, and 2,000 metres, often competing in three to seven races a day — the breakdown of energy systems is estimated best by averaging most of the races at two to four minutes in length. The percentage contribution of the energy pathways for dragon boating has been estimated in the chart that makes comparisons with other sports.

Now that the energy systems have been described, a brief look at muscle composition will show how the periodized dragon boat training program, to be outlined next, has resulted in over 1,000 world championship medals and has continued to produce world champions.

FAST AND SLOW TWITCH MUSCLES

≠ ≒

Are you a better 200-metre dragon boater or 2,000-metre dragon boater? Many people believe that having more fast- and slow-twitch muscle fibres may determine what distances dragon boaters excel at and how they respond to training.

Bundles of individual muscle fibres, or myocytes, make up the skeletal muscle. Each myocyte contains many myofibrils, strands of proteins (actin and myosin), that grab on to each other and pull. This activity shortens the muscle and causes muscle contraction.

Muscle fibres can be broken down into two main types: *slow twitch (Type I)* muscle fibres and *fast twitch (Type II)* muscle fibres. Fast twitch fibres can be further categorized into *Type IIa* and *Type IIb* fibres.

How muscles respond to training and physical activity are influenced by these muscle fibre distinctions. And, each fibre type is unique in its ability to contract in a certain way. Human muscles contain a genetically determined mixture of both slow and fast fibre types. On average, you have about 50 percent slow twitch and 50 percent fast twitch fibres in most of the muscles used for movement.

Slow Twitch (Type I)

The slow twitch muscles are more efficient at using oxygen to generate more fuel (ATP) for continuous, extended muscle contractions over a long time. They fire more slowly than fast twitch fibres and can last a long time before fatigue. Slow twitch fibres are beneficial in helping athletes run marathons or paddle for hours.

Fast Twitch (Type II)

Because fast twitch fibres use anaerobic metabolism to create fuel, they can generate short bursts of strength or speed much better than slow muscles. However, they fatigue more quickly. Although fast twitch fibres generally produce the same amount of force per contraction as slow muscles, they earn their name by firing more rapidly. Given this, more fast twitch fibres can be an asset to sprinters who need to quickly generate a lot of force.

Type IIa Fibres

A sub-category of fast twitch muscles are Type IIa fibres, also known as intermediate fast-twitch fibres. These can use both aerobic and anaerobic metabolism almost equally to create energy. In this way, they are a combination of Type I and Type II muscle fibres.

Type IIb Fibres

The second sub-category of fast twitch fibres are Type IIb fibres that use anaerobic metabolism to create energy. These are the "classic" fast twitch muscle fibres that produce quick, powerful bursts of speed. Of all the muscle fibre types, this one has the highest rate of contraction, or rapid firing. At the same time however, it has a much faster rate of fatigue and cannot last as long before rest is needed.

Fibre Type and Performance

Your muscle fibre type can play a part in determining which distances you are naturally good at or if you are fast or strong. Genetic makeup can determine the sport that is pursued by elite athletes. For example, Olympic sprinters have been shown to possess about 80 percent fast twitch fibres. Athletes who excel in marathons tend to have 80 percent slow twitch fibres.

The key is to determine what your strengths and weaknesses are by testing all physical parameters and training accordingly. Training programs that have been designed in this chapter will allow all beginner and elite dragon boaters to excel with high-intensity training. This is because *there is evidence that muscle fibre types, specifically Type IIb, can be changed into Type IIa with proper training*. Conditioning can improve personal performance.

This finding is important in the dragon boat world. You can train the fast-twitch, strong, powerful fibres to operate under both anaerobic, as well as aerobic, situations and create highly efficient power endurance muscle fibres.

TESTING

$$\neq \neq$$

Before the specifics of training are outlined, a brief testing regime with some standards has been put together for reference and comparison.

Testing

	MEN				WOMEN			
	Junior	Beginner	Intermediate	Elite	Junior	Beginner	Intermediate	Elite
Bench Press 100% BW (reps)	1	0	8	8-20	0	0	2-5	5-12
Bench Press 50% BW (reps)	10-20	10-20	30-50	50+	0-10	0-10	10-20	30+
Pull-ups (reps)	10-15	6-10	15-20	20-50	1-3	0	4-10	10-20
Reverse Pull-ups (reps)	10-15	0-10	15-30	30+	0-10	0-10	10-20	25+
Trap Bar Dead Lift 100% BW (reps)	0-15	0-15	15-30	30+	0-15	0-15	15-30	30+
1 mile run (min.)	7-8	7.5-8.5	6.5-7.5	5.5-6.5	7.5-8.5	8-9	7-8	6-7
Body Fat (%)	14-18	16-22	12-16	8-12	16-22	20-28	18-22	14-18
No Hold Sit-ups (reps)	0-15	0-5	15-30	30+	0-10	0-5	15-30	30+
1 arm-row R/L Avg. 1 min. (reps)	60 lbs 20	60 lbs 20	60 lbs 40	60 lbs 60+	40 lbs 20	40 lbs 20	40 lbs 40	40 lbs 60+
500 m Multistroke (time min.)	3:15 - 3:30	3:30 - 3:45	2:45 -3:15	2:11 -2:20	3:30 -3:45	3:45 - 4:00	3:00 - 3:30	2:30 -2:50

BW = Body Weight

R/L = Right/Left

Multistroke = Ergometer

Training Program

≠ ≠

Finally, what you have been waiting for — how to get better on the water by training hard off the water. Before piecing together the perfect program, you must understand your goals and the goals of your crew. Look at the season to come and schedule accordingly. Consider all the regattas, training camps, on-water practices, et cetera, so that the dry land strength and conditioning program can guarantee that you and your crew are strongest and fittest by the final regatta of the season. Too often, paddlers and coaches train hard all winter to peak at the start of the season as opposed to the end of the season. And, paddlers make great strength gains in the winter, then neglect strength training through the spring and summer months, only to start at their same strength level come the following year.

The program is designed to improve your strength and conditioning throughout the year so you peak at the end of the season and continue to improve every year going forward.[2] With this program, paddlers have seen their bench presses increase more than 300 percent in three years, pull-ups as much as 500 percent, with other lifts and exercises yielding similar results. These workouts can be done by anyone. The program is designed so that you can adapt at your own pace. There are no secrets; the harder you work and the more weight that you try to lift, the faster you will adapt and progress. You need to complete the specified sets, reps and times. The key, again, is to lift the heaviest weight possible for the reps given for a particular exercise. If the program is six sets of eight reps, the target should be within three reps of the given amount of reps on your last two sets. For example, on your 5th and 6th set, the expectation is that you squeeze out a minimum of five reps and a maximum of eight reps using the above example. This is an important rule because the program is designed for neural activation so that the nervous system fires more motor units that recruit more muscle fibres. These, in turn, make you, as a dragon boat paddler, stronger and assist in the ultimate goal of turning your Type IIa fibres into fatigue-resistant powerhouses. The program is periodized with the assumption that the season ends in September and begins in October, and that the big regatta is in August. The goal is identified at the top of each program. A proper warm-up and cool-down of an easy jog or bike ride is needed to get the blood through the muscles for quicker recovery.

Training: Phase 1

CLIENT:	You
PHASE:	1
LENGTH:	Oct.-Dec.
GOAL:	General Adaptation
LEGEND:	Paired = #'s
****Every workout begins with a 5-10 min. warm up****	
Try to add one LSD run on a convenient day.	

LSD = Running a Long Slow Distance at a moderate pace.

Training: Phase 1: Workout #1

Phase 1: Workout #1	Goal: A				
Exercise Order	Exercise	Sets	Reps	Tempo	Rest
1	DB Chest Press	8	10	20X	
1	Dead Lift	8	10	20X	
1	Shoulder Press	8	10	20X	
1	Bent Row	8	10	20X	
2	Run 2 min. on then 1 min. off x 7				
Full Body Stretch					

DB = Dumbbell
X = Full Speed

Training: Phase 1: Workout #2

Phase 1: Workout #2	Goal: A				
Exercise Order	Exercise	Sets	Reps	Tempo	Rest
1	Bench Press	8	15	20X	
1	Squats	8	15	20X	
1	Lateral/Front Raise	8	15	20X	
1	Lat Pulls	8	15	20X	
2	Run 1 min. on then 1 min. off x 7				
Full Body Stretch					

Training: Phase 1: Workout #3

Phase 1: Workout #3	Goal: A				
Exercise Order	Exercise	Sets	Reps	Tempo	Rest
1	Squat-Curl Press	8	30	20X	
1	Push-ups	8	30	20X	
1	Dumbbell Row	8	30	20X	
1	Back Fly	8	30	20X	
2	Run 1 min on 1 min ab exercise x 10				
Full Body Stretch					

Training: Phase 1: Workout #4

Phase 1: Workout #4	Goal: A	Circuit			
Exercise Order	Exercise	Sets	Reps	Tempo	Rest
1	Incline Dumbbell Press	8	20	20X	
1	Chin-ups	8	Max	X	
1	Standing Military	8	20	20X	
1	High Pull	8	20	20X	
2	Circuit 3 x 20 reps 1. Hamstring Tilt 2. V-twist 3. Squat Jumps 4. Russian Twist				
Full Body Stretch					

X = Full Speed

Training: Phase 1: Sample Week

Sample Week						
Monday	Tuesday	Wednesday	Thursday	Friday	Saturday	Sunday
1		2		3	LSD	

LSD = Running a Long Slow Distance at a moderate pace.

(left) Shoulder Press: Position dumbbells on each side of shoulders with elbows below wrists.

(right) Shoulder Press: Exhale and press dumbbells until arms are extended over head. Inhale as you lower the dumbbells.

Training: Phase 2

CLIENT:	You
PHASE:	2
LENGTH:	January
GOAL:	Adaptation 2
LEGEND:	Paired = #'s
****Every workout begins with a 5-10 min. warm up****	
Try to add one LSD run on a convenient day.	

LSD = Running a Long Slow Distance at a moderate pace.

Training: Phase 2: Workout #1

Phase 2: Workout #1	Goal: A				
Exercise Order	Exercise	Sets	Reps	Tempo	Rest
1	DB Chest Press	8	8	20X	
1	Dead Lift	8	8	20X	
1	Shoulder Press	8	8	20X	
1	Bent Row	8	8	20X	
2	Run 3 min. on 1 min. off x 7				
	Full Body Stretch				

DB = Dumbbell
X = Full Speed

Training: Phase 2: Workout #2

Phase 2: Workout #2	Goal: A				
Exercise Order	Exercise	Sets	Reps	Tempo	Rest
1	Bench Press	8	10	20X	
1	Squats	8	10	20X	
1	Lateral/Front Raise	8	10	20X	
1	Lat Pulls	8	10	20X	
2	Run 2 min. on 2 min. off x 7				
	Full Body Stretch				

X = Full Speed

Training: Phase 2: Workout #3

Phase 2: Workout #3	Goal: A				
Exercise Order	Exercise	Sets	Reps	Tempo	Rest
1	Squat-Curl Press	8	30	20X	
1	Push-ups	8	30	20X	
1	DB Row	8	30	20X	
1	Back Fly	8	30	20X	
2	Run 1 min. on 1 min. ab exercise x 10				
Full Body Stretch					

DB = Dumbbell
X = Full Speed

Training: Phase 2: Workout #4

Phase 2: Workout #4	Goal: A				
Exercise Order	Exercise	Sets	Reps	Tempo	Rest
1	Incline Dumbbell Press	8	7	X	
1	Chin-ups	8	7 max	X	
1	Standing Military	8	7	X	
1	High Pull	8	7	X	
2	Circuit 3 x 40 reps 1. Hamstring Tilt 2. V-twist 3. Squat Jumps 4. Russian Twist				
Full Body Stretch					

X = Full Speed

Training: Phase 2: Sample Week

Sample Week						
Monday	Tuesday	Wednesday	Thursday	Friday	Saturday	Sunday
1		2		3	LSD	

(left) Squats: With feet shoulder-width apart, hold the bar with an overhand grip as it rests on the shoulders.

(right) Squats: Inhale, contract abs, and bend knees until the thighs are horizontal to the floor. Return to start position and exhale at the end of the movement.

Photographs by Steven Ercolani

Training: Phase 3

CLIENT:	You
PHASE:	3
LENGTH:	February
GOAL:	HxS Adapt
LEGEND:	Paired = #'s
****Every workout begins with a 5-10 min. warm-up****	

HxS = Hypertrophy Strength Adaptation

Training: Phase 3: Workout #1

Phase 3: Workout #1	Goal: H				
Exercise Order	Exercise	Sets	Reps	Tempo	Rest
1	DB Chest Press	10	10	402	
1	Bent Row	10	10	402	
2	Decline Fly	3	10	402	
2	Seated Row	3	10	402	
3	Standing Shoulder Press	10	10	402	
3	Skipping	10	1 min	X	
Full Body Stretch					

DB = Dumbbell
Tempo – 1st number in seconds for up; 2nd number is pause; 3rd number in seconds for concentric
X = Full Speed

Training: Phase 3: Workout #2

Phase 3: Workout #2	Goal: H	Rest 1 min. after each group			
Exercise Order	Exercise	Sets	Reps	Tempo	Rest
1	Dead Lift	6	10	20X	
1	Biceps Curl	6	10	301	
2	Front Squats - Press	6	10	20X	
2	Triceps Ext	6	10	301	
3	Dumbbell Squat-Calf Raise	4	10	20X	
3	Stiff-Leg Curl Press	4	10	201	
3	Core	4	1 min.	X	1 min.
Full Body Stretch					

X = Full Speed

Training: Phase 3: Workout #3

Phase 3: Workout #3	Goal: HxS				
Exercise Order	Exercise	Sets	Reps	Tempo	Rest
1	Incline Press	4	6	20X	
1	Weighted Chins	4	6	20X	1 min.
2	Neutral Press	4	6	20X	
2	T-Bar Seated Row	4	6	20X	1 min.
3	Decline Press	4	6	20X	
3	Bent Over Back Fly	4	6	20X	1 min.
4	Cable Twist	4	6	20X	
4	Back Extension	4	12	20X	
4	Weighted V-Tw-V-Up	4	12	X	
Full Body Stretch					

X = Full Speed

Training: Phase 3: Workout #4

Phase 3: Workout #4	Goal: HxS				
Exercise Order	Exercise	Sets	Reps	Tempo	Rest
1	Dead Lift	4	6	20X	
1	Military Press	4	6	20X	1 min.
2	Lunges	4	6	20X	
2	Front Raises	4	6	20X	1 min.
3	Overhead Deep Squat	4	6	20X	
3	Shrug-Calf Raise	4	6	20X	1 min.
4	Skipping	4	45 sec.	X	
4	Hand Stabilizer	4	1.5 min		
4	Medicine Ball Smashes	4	6	X	
Full Body Stretch					

X = Full Speed

Training: Phase 3: Sample Week

Sample Week						
Monday	Tuesday	Wednesday	Thursday	Friday	Saturday	Sunday
1		2		3	LSD	

LSD = Running a Long Slow Distance at a moderate pace.

Photographs by Steven Ercolani

One-Arm Row: With your back level to the floor and one hand on the bench for support, start with the weight down by your side.

One-Arm Row: Exhale, lift dumbbell, and concentrate on using your back and shoulder muscles, rather than biceps.

Training: Phase 4

CLIENT:	You
PHASE:	4
LENGTH:	March
GOAL:	General Strength
LEGEND:	Paired = #'s
****Every workout begins with a 5-10 min. warm up****	
Try to add one LSD run on a convenient day.	

LSD = Running a Long Slow Distance at a moderate pace.

Training: Phase 4: Workout #1

Phase 4: Workout #1	Goal: A				
Exercise Order	Exercise	Sets	Reps	Tempo	Rest
1	Bench Press	10	6	X	
1	Deep Squats	10	6	X	
1	Push Press	10	6	X	
1	Weighted Chin-ups	10	6	X	
1	Anaerobic activity at 100% for 45 sec., i.e., burpees, sprints, row, etc.				
Full Body Stretch					

Training: Phase 4: Workout #2

Phase 4: Workout #2	Goal: A				
Exercise Order	Exercise	Sets	Reps	Tempo	Rest
1	DB Neutral	8	8	XXX	
1	Dead Lifts	8	8	XXX	
1	Back Fly	8	8	XXX	
1	Bent Row	8	8	XXX	
1	Core for 1 min.				
1	Full Body Stretch				

DB = Dumbbell

Training: Phase 4: Workout #3

Phase 4: Workout #3	Goal: A				
Exercise Order	Exercise	Sets	Reps	Tempo	Rest
1	High Pull	10	6	X	
1	Dumbbell Press	10	6	X	
1	Dumbbell Row	10	6	X	
1	Lateral Raise	10	6	X	
1	1 min. sprint x 10 at 100%				
1	Full Body Stretch				

Training: Phase 4: Workout #4

Phase 4: Workout #4	Goal: A				
Exercise Order	Exercise	Sets	Reps	Tempo	Rest
1	Seated Row	8	7	X	
1	Dumbbell Shoulder Press	8	7	X	
1	Dead Lifts	8	7	X	
1	Decline Bench Press	8	7	X	
2	Jumping Jacks or skipping 2 min.				
Full Body Stretch					

Training: Phase 4: Sample Week

Sample Week						
Monday	Tuesday	Wednesday	Thursday	Friday	Saturday	Sunday
1		2		3		

Bench Press: Use an overhand grip wider than shoulder width on the barbell. Inhale and lower the bar to the chest.

Bench Press: Exhale and extend arms.

Training: Phase 5

CLIENT:	You
PHASE:	5
LENGTH:	April
GOAL:	M-Strength
LEGEND:	Paired = #'s
****Every workout begins with a 5-10 min. warm-up****	
Try to add one LSD run on a convenient day.	

LSD = Running a Long Slow Distance at a moderate pace.

Training: Phase 5: Workout #1

Phase 5: Workout #1	Goal: S		REST 1 min. after each group.		
Exercise Order	Exercise	Sets	Reps	Tempo	Rest
1	Bench Press	10	5,5,5,3,3,1,1,1,1,1	20X	
1	Weighted Chin-ups	10	5,5,5,3,3,1,1,1,1,1	20X	
1	Front Raise	10	5,5,5,3,3,1,1,1,1,1	20X	
1	Deep Squat	10	5,5,5,3,3,1,1,1,1,1	20X	

Training: Phase 5: Workout #2

Phase 5: Workout #2	Goal: S		REST 1 min. after each group.		
Exercise Order	Exercise	Sets	Reps	Tempo	Rest
1	Dead Lift	10	5,5,5,3,3,1,1,1,1,1	20X	
1	Decline Bench	10	5,5,5,3,3,1,1,1,1,1	20X	
1	Bent Row	10	5,5,5,3,3,1,1,1,1,1	20X	
1	Military Press	10	5,5,5,3,3,1,1,1,1,1	20X	

Training: Phase 5: Workout #3

Phase 5: Workout #3	Goal: S		REST 1 min. after each group.		
Exercise Order	Exercise	Sets	Reps	Tempo	Rest
1	Back Squat	10	5,5,5,3,3,1,1,1,1,1	20X	
1	DB Press	10	5,5,5,3,3,1,1,1,1,1	20X	
1	Seated Row	10	5,5,5,3,3,1,1,1,1,1	20X	
1	DB Squat	10	5,5,5,3,3,1,1,1,1,1	20X	

DB = Dumbbell

Training: Phase 5: Workout #4

Phase 5: Workout #4	Goal: Velocity	REST 1 min. after each group.			
Exercise Order	Exercise	Sets	Reps	Tempo	Weight
1	Bench Press	3	5,4,3,	XXX	40% RM
1	Weighted Chin-ups	3	5,4,3	XXX	40% RM
1	Standing Shoulder	3	5,4,3	XXX	40% RM
1	Deep Squat	3	5,4,3	XXX	40% RM
1	Dumbbell Press	3	5,4,3	XXX	40% RM
1	Bent Row	3	5,4,3	XXX	40% RM
1	Back Fly	3	5,4,3	XXX	40% RM
1	Dead Lift	3	5,4,3	XXX	40% RM

RM= Rep Max

1. This workout is designed to move a light weight (40% of max.) as fast as possible for minimum reps.
2. Make sure that you do not fatigue yourself. Everything should feel extremely light.
3. The goal is to recruit fast-twitch fibres without the extreme load of doing maximum effort lifts.
4. Workouts 1, 2 and 3 are designed to maximize strength. The high sets are strictly for warm-up and activation, building up to max weight. An example of the weights you should be lifting follow below.

Training: Phase 5: Workout #4: Sets Example

70 lb for 3 reps (40% RM)
95 lb for 3 reps (50% RM)
115 lb for 1 rep (60% RM)
135 lb for 1 rep (70% RM)
155 lb for 1 rep (80% RM)
175 lb for 1 rep (90% RM)
190 lb for 1 rep (103% RM)

This setup is for someone who lifts 185 lb for their 1 rep max (RM). 45 lbs for 3 sets of 5 reps (25% RM)

Training: Phase 5: Sample Week

Sample Week						
Monday	Tuesday	Wednesday	Thursday	Friday	Saturday	Sunday
1		2		3	LSD	

LSD = Running a Long Slow Distance at a moderate pace.

Training: Phase May-June

CLIENT:	You
PHASE:	May-June
LENGTH:	4 weeks
GOAL:	Main./Spec.Endurance
LEGEND:	Paired = #'s

Training: Phase May-June: Workout #1

Phase May-June: Workout #1	Goal: M/SE									
Exercise Order	Exercise	Sets	Reps	Tempo	Rest	RUN 1				
1	Dumbbell Press	6	5	X		Interval				
1	Straight Arm Pulls	6	5	X		W-up	On	Off	Sets	Rest
1	High Power Pull	6	5	X		5	4	1	6	0
1	Weighted Chins	6	5	X						
2	Bench Press	3	8	X						
2	Dead Lift	3	8	X						
2	Bent Row	3	8	X						
3	Seated Row	4	2 min.	X						
3	Push-ups	4	2 min.	X		RUN 2				
3	Jump Squats	4	2 min.	X		Type= Interval at 85%				
						W-up	On	Off	Sets	Rest
						5	20s	20s	20	

Training: Phase May-June: Workout #2

Phase May-June: Workout #2	Goal: M								
Exercise Order	Exercise	Sets	Reps	Tempo					
1	Bench Press	4	4	X					
1	Single Arm Row	4	4	X					
1	Squats	4	4	X					
1	Back Fly	4	4	X	RUN 3				
2	Push-Press	5	50	X	Type= Interval at 100%				
2	Reverse Pull Ups	5	max	X	W-up	On	Off	Sets	Rest
2	Dumbbell Neutral Press	5	50	X	5	2	4	7	0
2	Front/Lateral Raise	5	50	X					

Training: Phase May-June: Sample Week

Sample Week						
Monday	Tuesday	Wednesday	Thursday	Friday	Saturday	Sunday
1/R1	Paddle	Paddle	2/R2	Paddle	Paddle	

These workouts are designed to maximize all strength systems within the season.

Training: Phase July-August

CLIENT:	You
PHASE:	July/August
LENGTH:	4 weeks
GOAL:	Peak
LEGEND:	Paired = #'s

Phase July-August: Workout #1

Phase July-Aug.: Workout #1	Goal: M/S				
Exercise Order	Exercise	Sets	Reps	Tempo	Rest
1	Bench Press	7	3	X	
1	Bent Row	7	3	X	
1	Dead Lift	7	3	X	
1	Push Press	7	3	X	
2	Neutral Press	4	5	X	
2	Dumbbell Row	4	5	X	
2	Dumbbell Squat	4	5	X	
2	Back Fly	4	30	X	
2	Lateral/Front Raise	4	5	X	
2	Russian Twist	4	30	X	

X = Full Speed

Training: Phase July-August: Workout #2

Phase July-Aug.: Workout #2	Goal: M				
Exercise Order	Exercise	Sets	Reps	Tempo	Rest
1	Bench Press	5	2	X	
1	Dumbbell Press	5	100	X	
1	Seated Row	5	2	X	
1	Dumbbell Row	5	100	X	
1	Dead-Lift	5	2	X	
2	Jump-Squats	5	100	X	
2	Shoulder Press	5	4	X	
2	Front Raise	5	100	X	

X = Full Speed

Elite paddlers jog in Penang, Malaysia, as part of their pre-race warm-up on Day Four of the 2008 Club Crew World Championships.

Phase July-August: Run #1

RUN 1				
Type= Interval 100%				
W-up	On	Off	Sets	Rest
5	1	3	10	0

Do Core at least 2x a week on free time for 15-20 min.

Training: Phase July-August: Run #2

RUN 2				
Type= Interval at 85%				
W-up	On	Off	Sets	Rest
5	4	2	8	

Do Core at least 2x a week on free time for 15-20 min.

Training: Phase July-August: Run #3

RUN 3				
Type= Interval at 100%				
W-up	On	Off	Sets	Rest
5	30s	15s	30	0

Do Core at least 2x a week on free time for 15-20 min.

Training: Phase July-August: Sample Week

SAMPLE WEEK						
Monday	Tuesday	Wednesday	Thursday	Friday	Saturday	Sunday
1/R1	Paddle	Paddle	2/R2	Paddle	Paddle	

CONCLUSION

These workouts are designed to peak for the big regatta in August. Adjustments can be made so that the peak period matches your dragon boat racing schedule.

In closing, the bottom line to dry land training is to set your goals and plan to peak when it counts, using a proven system or conditioning coach. Before you embark on this or any other training program, you should consult your family doctor.

NOTES

1. D. Matthews and E. Fox, *The Physiological Basis of Physical Education and Athletics* (Philadelphia: W.B. Saunders, 1988).

2. **Editor's Note:** For descriptions of the exercises, refer to "Internet Resources" in this book or to the ATP (Athletes Training Professionals) website (*www.torontoathlete.com*). Jamie Hollins is the strength and conditioning director of ATP in Pickering, Ontario.

SOURCES

Fox, Edward L. *The Physiological Basis for Exercise and Sport.* Boston: McGraw-Hill, 1997.

Fox, Edward L., Merle L. Foss, and Steven J. Ketevian. *Fox's Physiological Basis for Exercise and Sport*, 5th ed. Boston: McGraw-Hill, 1993.

Matthews, D., and Edward L. Fox. *The Physiological Basis of Physical Education and Athletics.* Philadelphia: W.B. Saunders, 1988.

4

Drumming and Steering

Matt Robert

龙　　　船

The presence of drums is a Chinese tradition that has been maintained in the modern sport of dragon boating. The drums are crafted from wood and covered with leather that is forged with iron hardware.

DRUMMING

≠ ≯

Racing to the sound of a drum, matching one's paddling stroke to the rhythm of a teammate pounding on a drum, is certainly unique in the sport of modern boat racing. The drum and the actual act of drumming are important ingredients of a competitive or elite team's chances of success. The International Dragon Boat Federation has specific rules; drummers must actively drum for all but the first 50 metres of a race. Failure to demonstrate active drumming can result in a time penalty. This might seem like a simple enough task; however, the role of the drummer is much more complex, making the actual drumming seem like an afterthought.

85

More than just a "hood ornament," the drummer calls the race plan and encourages paddlers at the Marilyn Bell Park course in Toronto, Ontario.

The Elite-Crew Drummer

The first point is that teams need to use their drummers. I have seen crews, racing at the world level, barely using their drummers and relying on the steerspersons to make all the calls. This is a waste of one teammate (the only circumstance when I would discourage the active role of a drummer is an emergency replacement situation that requires the use of a spare). The calls that drummers make are always scripted; they need to use common calls, at common times, using a common tone of voice. In combination, these command tactics definitely put teams in their comfort zone. Replacement drummers should be given strict parameters on what they can say and only when signalled by the steersperson.

Spare drummers aside, the number one criterion of the ideal drummer is body weight. Personality, race experience, voice projection, tactical knowledge, and motivational skills are all important but, if a team is asked to carry an extra 60 kilograms or more at the bow of the boat, that team will be at a great disadvantage. Imagine placing a 60-kilogram dumbbell at the front of the boat.

In competitive rowing, the coxswain has a similar role to that of the drummer in a dragon boat, but with the additional responsibility of steering. Competitive rowing teams never use

85-kilogram coxswains and justify their weight by the coxswain's unmatched motivational skills. In fact, rowing has maximum weight requirements for coxswains — 55 kilograms for men and 50 kilograms for women. My ideal drummer, male and female, weighs between 45 and 50 kilograms (and, yes, that is soaking wet!)

The second most important quality has two parts: knowledge and confidence. Confidence, in the absence of knowledge, is simply arrogance. Knowledge, without a confident voice, is a silent voice. When a confident and knowledgeable drummer speaks, paddlers respond as a unit. The only way to increase knowledge is to study, experience, and live the sport. The best drummers I know have spent many years paddling, and have coached, steered, and even refereed. The drummer must know the rules of racing inside out, understand technique, and relate to the pain that paddlers experience.

Race Strategy

During a typical race, the drummer plays a key role for the team. The drummer, steersperson, and coach should pre-determine the dry land and on-water warm-up regimen. This routine is determined early in the season (but never set in stone) and the drummer must take an active role in the warm-up. Having the drummer lead this pre-race activity immediately places the athletes' attention on the drummer's voice.

Before the warm-up, the drummer and steersperson need to strategize about the race. A good drummer takes notice of water depths along the racecourse. Knowledge of shallow spots can change a team's strategy and, ultimately, the outcome of a race. Drummers need to know about lane advantages and how to handle different types of wind. With wide lanes, one side might be deeper or more sheltered from the wind. The drummer will help pick the team's starting point in its lane and the desired racing line. Good drummers can change any part of a pre-determined strategy on the fly and with confidence.

Drummers help with the loading of the boat and keep an eye on how it is sitting in the water. Again, they need to be able to make quick decisions that go against the game plan. Crews that are used to training in a specific boat, with a specific line up, might need to re-shuffle the seating assignment to balance the boats provided at the race site. It is important to leave this responsibility with the drummer and steersperson rather than any of the paddlers. Paddlers simply need to focus on the

Photograph by Jan Oakley

Some crews trivialize the role of drummers, but their roles in calling out commands in precise cadence with the paddling rate, providing encouragement, and relaying commands from the steersperson are crucial. The drummer for Halifax's Dragon Beast crew proves her worth.

physically monumental task ahead. Trying to figure out the perfect boat balance will weaken a paddler's focus.

The drummer works with the steersperson to bring the boat to the desired starting position. Again, the paddlers in the boat should be focused on the race and not on positioning the boat. They need to know and feel that the boat is under absolute control,

even in extreme circumstances. Both the drummer and steersperson will ask for assistance from their paddlers to attain the proper starting position.

Once the race is underway, the drummer needs to follow the start and communicate with the crew into race pace. Good drummers will recognize a flawed start and take action. A pre-determined plan will have been set for all negative circumstances,

Photograph by Jens Ronneberger

The drum is considered, by some, the heartbeat of the dragon. The modern dragon boat, with 20 paddlers, has the drum and drummer at the front. Traditional dragon boats with 40 to 50 paddlers have the drum positioned in the middle of the boat.

such as bad starts, being behind early, bad timing, flawed pace, et cetera. Although the steersperson is in control of the boat direction, the drummer may signal the steersperson to move. For example, the drummer might want to steer away from a competing team that is trying to gain an advantage by wash riding. Or, the drummer might see that the steersperson has been distracted and has lost the racing line, all to say that the drummer helps steer the team.

Depending on the crew, a drummer can talk a team through an entire race or say the bare minimum. Knowing what motivates a crew takes time and acute attention during practices and races. Whether or not the drummer is the decision-maker on the boat, all tactical calls during the race should be

Photograph by Heather Maclaren

A Junior team at the Rio Tinto Alcan Dragon Boat Festival in Vancouver, British Columbia, glams it up. Creative team names, and thematic clothing and accessories contribute to team spirit.

Photograph by Jan Oakley

Active drumming requires that the drum be clearly struck with the drumstick at short, regular intervals. This rule is applied at traditional and international competitions.

called out by the drummer. This is where voice projection and clarity need to be perfect. The language used in a race must be rehearsed; good drummers do not change the way they call a finish from race to race.

Aside from studying the racecourse, helping manage the seating assignments, lining up the boat, calling the start and transition, actively drumming, and making decisions on the fly, the drummer should also retain as much information from the race as possible. Making improvements, both for individuals and the team, comes from evaluating mistakes. The drummer should remember all the moments of weakness and review them with the coaching staff.

The Recreational-Team Drummer

I have outlined the characteristics of an elite drummer knowing that only a small portion of dragon boaters worldwide fall into the elite category. Most dragon boat teams are in the recreational category where participation is more important than winning. For the recreational dragon boat team, the drummer's body weight is of no importance; in this division, it is all about attitude. The recreational drummer needs to be an outgoing spirit who wants to stay positive even if the team is losing by several boat lengths. Some festivals even encourage their drummers to show some originality in their creative costumes and props.

STEERING

≠ ≢

Like the drummer, the steersperson plays an important part in a dragon boat team's success or failure. I have seen steers clearly win races for their crews by making

smart decisions with their racing lines and calls. They have a unique perspective and feel on the dragon boat. More noticeably, however, are races that are clearly lost by the steerspersons.

Safety First

Before looking at the qualities of an elite steersperson, I would like to point out some basic safety guidelines. The most important realization for a steer is the immense weight and momentum of a dragon boat. The average dragon boat crew, in a standard racing boat, weighs approximately 1,800 kilograms. A crew of heavy men can be close to 2,275 kilograms. And, if an older style of boat is used, the crew and boat can weigh over 3,400 kilograms.

One person is responsible for steering and directing over 1,800 kilograms, and there are no mechanical brakes! To control the weight and momentum of the boat, the steer should be physically fit. I have seen many people who do not meet this requirement steer dragon boats; this is seen extensively around the world. Steering a boat, in a straight line and under ideal conditions, can be easy and can instill a false sense of security for a steersperson with limited physical strength. Steers need to be strong to manoeuvre the boat quickly in emergency situations and in adverse

Photograph by Jan Oakley

The response of the boat to the steering oar is opposite to the direction of the oar grip. If the steersperson pulls the oar grip right, or into the boat, the boat will turn left. If it is pushed out, or left, the boat turns right.

weather. I remember steering a boat in Florida when a large powerboat, making large rolling waves, flew by our crew. I needed to act quickly to point the bow of the boat directly into the waves. I had little time to change direction and used all of my strength to deepen the steering oar, twist it, and pull up hard on the U-bolt. We hit the waves head on, took in half a boat of water, but stayed afloat. Had we been hit by the waves from the side, our boat would have rolled over.

Steering in heavy crosswinds demands constant pressure on the steering arm, thus requiring strength as well. Steering can be as easy as holding the steering oar with one hand, barely thinking about it, or it can require both hands, two solid feet, and decent strength.

Before letting their teams embark at practices or races, the steers are responsible for several safety checks.

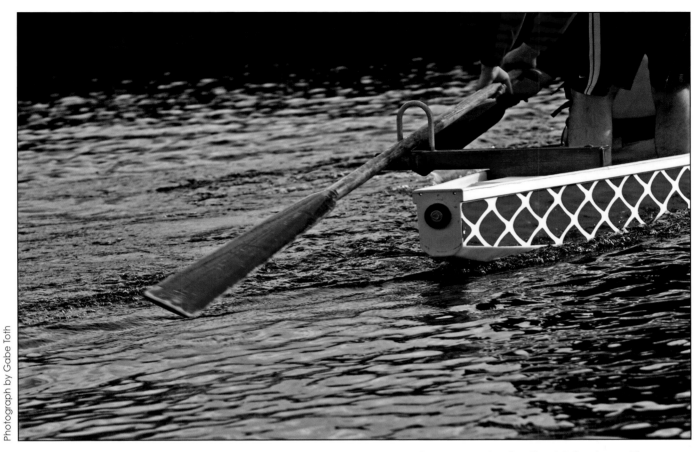

The U-bolt is affixed to the left side of the steering deck as the fulcrum point for the 10-foot oar. The steersperson makes all turns and course corrections slowly and incrementally.

First, the steer should check the integrity of the boat to make sure that it is sound. The steering arm must be solidly connected to the boat and must not be cracked or rotted. Safety equipment is required. Depending on local rules, supplies typically include two bailers, a thirty-metre throw line, flashlight, whistle, and water-sealed communication device for calling 9-1-1.

Every team should have a safety plan for boat emergencies. If a boat capsizes, the steersperson and drummer need to be the two lead people. The reason they need to be in control is that the most dangerous situation occurs when a boat capsizes and turns upside down, and paddlers are trapped or caught under the seats. Although the drummer and steer may suffer injuries, they are not likely to be caught under the boat during a flip. That is why both drummer and steer are assigned this responsibility to work as a team to control the situation.

Photograph by Derek Griffiths

Many races are won or lost through the skill and daring of the steersperson, especially in the 2,000-metre event that has several turns. Ideally, the steering oar is held out of the water as much as possible to reduce drag.

The Biggest Mistake

Before getting into racing, I would like to point out the biggest mistake that steers make; that is, tying down, or lashing, the steering oar to the U-bolt.

When someone is learning how to steer, the tied-down oar, compared to a free one, provides an easier learning experience. In fact, it is a good idea to start with the oar tied down, like having a training wheel. Sooner, rather than later, the training wheel

Photograph by Heather Maclaren

At the False Creek Women's Regatta in Vancouver, the steersperson follows the "rules of the road" to bring his team back to the loading area.

needs to come off. With the oar tied down to the U-bolt, you limit the types of turns and different pressure points you can achieve. The steer must have the liberty to submerge the steering oar as much, or as little, as needed. Tying down the oar also prevents the steer from using the top corners of the U-bolt for tight turns.

Steering Stance

Novices often ask about the ideal standing positions on the boat. The first thing I tell them is to learn how to steer from all parts of the back deck and in all sorts of stances. Often, steers are challenged to balance the boat when there is an uneven number of paddlers or right-left distribution of weight. Learning how to steer from different angles will also give a different

Photograph by Matt Robert

The steersperson must maintain total control by being aware of race conditions and other boats, manoeuvring safely and effectively, ensuring silence among the paddlers, and providing clear boat commands.

feel of the oar and make steers better equipped to handle new or unfamiliar boats, often the case for North American crews racing abroad.

What Makes a Good Steersperson

Just like the drummer, body weight is a huge portion of the equation. When I see 90-kilogram steers, myself included, I see too much dead weight. There is no elite crew in the world that would not *feel* the difference between a 90-kilogram and 70-kilogram steersperson. The ideal steer should weigh around 65 to 70 kilograms, and have above-average strength for that weight.

Top steers have an acute sensitivity to boat speed and water depth, and a knowledge of wash riding. Being able to feel boat speed will allow a good steer to make appropriate calls. It is much smarter to call for a pickup when you need one, rather than at a predetermined point in the race. Looking for and recognizing water depth also keeps you alert to make the necessary calls.

Although not permitted under IDBF and Dragon Boat Canada (DBC) Rules of Racing, learning, and mastering wash riding is a core element of steering. I know of no other sport where the "drag effect"

and its impact on speed are as powerful. Although I am not aware of any research on this topic, the crew saves energy if it is riding on the wake of a leading boat. Wash riding is not permitted in dragon boat racing except in 2,000-metre races. Steerpersons are expected to stay in the middle of their lanes and move in either direction if asked by the referee. Despite this rule, however, wash riding is a reality at all levels of racing. It is also a great tool during practices with multiple teams. A slower crew can challenge the stronger one by riding on the wash.

CONCLUSION

The strategy for boat calls that are initiated by the drummer or steersperson is specific to each team. Some steers call all the shots with drummers repeating, or vice versa. When making calls, steers need to keep a feel for direction and have a good sense of the racing lines of crews around them, especially in 2,000-metre races. The drummer and steer can help win or lose a race and, just like paddling, the only way to get better is to practise, observe, and adapt.

5

Dragon Boat Coaching

Kamini Jain

龙　船

To coach effectively, you must challenge your paddlers in an enjoyable environment. In addition, the paddlers must see that their efforts are creating gains. Even with the diversity of dragon boat teams and dragon boat paddlers, most commit to this sport with the desire to be challenged at some level and see improvement. If paddling on your team is both enjoyable and challenging, your team will grow as word spreads and paddlers introduce their friends and colleagues to the team. In this chapter, I will discuss the groundwork for creating challenges, the structure for creating improvement and some ideas for creating a constructive, enjoyable environment.

CREATING CHALLENGES: TEAM MANDATE AND GOAL-SETTING
≠ ⧣

Team Mandate

Some dragon boat teams train and race with the mandate of racing with the fastest crew always, others participate for purely social or support reasons, and most are somewhere along a continuum in between. Understanding and defining the mandate of the team is an essential starting point for all coaches. From my experience, this mandate must be arrived at by the paddlers as a whole. What are they getting into with this team? How do they want the team run? What factors are important in choosing which team members are in the boat on the starting line? A mission statement serves well as a foundation and reminder of team objectives. For example: "The Calgary Dragons[1] aim to nurture camaraderie and sportsmanship among youth paddlers by encouraging participation and racing for every team member."

Before accepting the position as coach of a team, an individual must ensure that his or her own coaching objectives are in line with the objectives of the team. For example, a coach who values winning above all else will not be a good fit for the Calgary Dragons who value participation first.

Goal-Setting

Once the mandate is defined, the coach and team can determine their goals. These can include such endeavours as increasing membership numbers, gaining a corporate sponsor, and, of course, some performance goals. For most teams, goals for the present or upcoming season should be accompanied by longer term goals to ensure

Dragon boating has been the most positive team sport experience in my life. It is a sport where those, who work together in perfect harmony toward a common goal, can achieve success at whatever level they set their sights on.
— Gord Ramsey, Winnipeg, Manitoba

perpetuity of the team and year-to-year progress of paddlers. Goal-setting requires answers to such questions as what race results are we aiming for this season? What about next season? Do we have sufficient paddlers and funds to reach these goals?

Once set, goals need be reassessed periodically, as some will be met, some surpassed and others will lag behind. Periodic goal assessment will make sure goals stay challenging and, if they are not being met, training methods or goals will be corrected as required. Aiming for and meeting goals in a structured training environment creates the enjoyment and motivation a coach wishes to provide his or her athletes. Most important to consider when goal-setting is that the objectives defined in the team mandate and the goals set must be in line. As an example, for the Calgary Dragons to set the seasonal, or even two-year, plan to be a top three team in Canada may not be realistic considering their mandate of participation first.

STRUCTURING TO CREATE IMPROVEMENT

Once the team's mandate and goals are understood, the coach must plan how these goals are going to be sought. Creating structure for the season is imperative. The most comprehensive plan, which is, ideally, defined before the start of the season, includes a seasonal training plan, a team selection process, a practice structure, and a technical plan. Throughout the season, race day plans and race plans will need to be developed.

Season Planning

A seasonal plan marks out the season day by day, taking into account the goals of the team and the coach's feeling of what is required at different parts of the season to achieve these. My suggestion as a starting point for a seasonal plan is to:

* Make a calendar;
* Enter target regattas;
* Enter team selection events;
* Structure training around entered dates.

The fourth step is the challenging one for the coach. The amount of detail involved here is dependent upon the loftiness of the team's goals and its current performance level. A team with goals of great improvement or high achievement will need more structured and scientific training than a purely recreational team, largely because these teams will practise more often and gains will be harder to achieve. Most dragon boat teams are more on the recreational side of competitive sport and train two to three times a week, four to seven months a year. They will improve with a simple plan that addresses the key requirements of 500-metre racing. These I will address briefly (detailed physiological training principles are beyond the scope of this chapter and can be found from many other resource materials, such as coaching manuals or various training books on the market).

Types of training to address key requirements of 500-metre racing:

True Aerobic Base Work:
Low-intensity, long-duration work pieces to build base endurance that provides paddlers with the fitness to work at higher intensities and recover between pieces, workouts, and races. These pieces also provide an environment for working on technique at low speeds. A coach can work this facet with pieces longer than six minutes at a steady intensity, with short rest times. The intensity for this work is not physically draining, although the paddler will feel tired by the end of the workout.

Mid-Intensity Base Work:
Middle intensity, middle duration work pieces that allow the paddler to work on technique at a moderate speed and have the psychological feel of doing a tough, draining workout. These pieces are longer than race distance and done at sub-maximal intensity. Each piece would create some fatigue.

Above Race-Pace Intensity:
These pieces are shorter than race distance and are completed at an intensity higher than race pace. Paddlers should be given a lot of rest between these pieces to allow for repeats at a similarly high intensity. These pieces teach paddlers to maintain their technique at a high pace and increase their power output in

order to increase, over time, race pace. Psychologically, they give paddlers the confidence that they can work at a high intensity and maintain their composure and technique. Start work should be integrated into these pieces.

Lactic Acid Tolerance:
These workouts are intense with short rest periods and are used to teach the paddlers to create, metabolize and tolerate the painful products of high-intensity work. These workouts create a lot of fatigue and should not be done often, regardless of the level of the team (once every two weeks is enough). A coach should read more about these specific kinds of workouts before integrating them into the training plan as they are a waste of good energy if not done effectively.

Race Pace:
These workouts are done at race pace over durations shorter than a race. The goal of these workouts is to get the paddlers comfortable with paddling at race pace, technically, physically,

and emotionally. Sufficient rest should be provided such that the paddlers can reach race pace each piece. In my experience, these pieces are best started with a dead start as a realistic race pace is difficult to pinpoint using a running start (gradual build to pace). Usually, with a running start, the pace found will be too slow. On a good program, your team will not do 500 metres at its potential until the paddlers are peaked, rested and lined up next to other competitors on race day. So, to find the correct pace, you have to do pieces shorter than race distance.

The simplest way of putting all these pieces together is working through the season, starting at the beginning of the list, and getting good base work done with true aerobic base work and mid-intensity base work. Then, as the season progresses, replacing some of these with a few above race-pace intensity workouts with a lactic acid tolerance workout every two weeks. When race season is underway, add some race pace work. At this time, mid- and low-intensity work would be limited to an occasional warm-up or cool-down piece for a crew that trains two to three times per week. Working backward is always a good

Photograph by Normand Beaulieu

Canadian Grand Dragon Women warm up at the 2007 World Dragon Boat Racing Championships in Sydney, Australia, after a year-long process of selection and training.

approach: What skills do my paddlers need to have on a specific race day and what route do I need to take to get them there on this day?

One concept to incorporate into your seasonal plan to get the most gains is to progressively overload and then rest your paddlers. The idea is that if an athlete works harder, gains are higher but so is fatigue. So working a paddler hard and then allowing a period of decreased work, or recovery, leads them to greater improvements over the season than a constant work load. To do this, divide your plan into segments (one week is simplest) and cycle through work loads: medium → hard → easy week, then back to medium. In addition, before major regattas or trials, have a medium week and then an easy week, and follow a major regatta with an easy week. Again, it works well to work backward. Look at your calendar of events, put in the intensities required surrounding the regattas and then work back through time to the pre-season.

Team Selection Processes

Teams run much smoother when everyone knows ahead of time what must be done in order to be in the crew on race day. As the coach, having your plan set and communicated will save you angst and drama when crew selection time comes. To set these requirements, look first at the team mandate. What is important to the team? Participation? Results? A combination? Next, what resources do you have at hand to assist in your selection? The best kinds of selection are measurable and, hence, purely objective: time trials if small boats are available and trained in, ergometer tests, attendance records, and fitness tests. Other selection parameters will be subjective like attitude and technique. A coach's best friend to improve the technique of his or her crew and to tackle the subjective nature of assessing and selecting based on dragon boat technique is a video camera. Video footage taken throughout the season gives the coach and paddler an opportunity to address technical weaknesses and gives the paddler an idea of how they are doing relative to others.

Practice Structure

Each practice should have a training goal in accordance with the timing on the seasonal plan, whether it is base fitness, pacing, or one of the other facets of training. The practice must be planned to address this goal. Having a practice planned out beforehand ensures the goal is addressed and the workout is streamlined and disciplined with coach and paddlers

Dry land warm-ups raise the heart rate before a race or practice. A team takes advantage of running up and down the hill at the Ottawa Dragon Boat Festival.

knowing what comes next. An unstructured practice can easily become derailed by chatty, distracted, and/or confused paddlers. As a coach, there are so many requirements to running a smooth practice; knowing the specific work intervals in advance allows you to focus on other tasks to get the best out of the team.

Warm-Up

First, every practice must have a warm-up. Many crews do a group dry land warm-up, which is good for both team unity and race day preparation, where the on-water warm-up time is usually so short that a thorough dry land warm-up is required. This warm-up should involve both cardiovascular work and stretching and can be fine-tuned throughout the season.

On the water, a warm-up is also required. My suggestion is to start with easy paddling, getting the paddlers to increase their range of motion and gel as a team with some segment paddling (for example, odd-numbered seats only then even-numbered seats

Side stretches of the lats, the muscles on each side of the back, help prevent injuries.

On-the-water warm-ups help paddlers stretch out and focus as a team at the beginning of a practice and before a race.

> There is nothing like the feel of that paddle in your hands, the sound of the drum, the call of your sterns man and the spray of cool lake water to make you feel alive.
> — Laura Newman, London, Ontario

or front half of the boat only, then back half of the boat). Then, increase paddling intensity gradually and allow for realistic attainment of requested intensity. If you ask your team to paddle race pace after a short low-intensity warm-up, they will paddle slower than their real race pace. So, structure the warm-up so if you ask for a fast pace, they have done enough work to be prepared to reach that speed. This boosts morale. In the warm-up, do at least one piece at the intensity required in the workout. If the team can't obtain the intensity, they're not warmed up yet. Allow sufficient rest in the warm-up to meet these objectives.

Workout

For the workout, you will need to have planned the structure: How many pieces? How long? How much rest? Do the pieces have starts or not? If you are doing pieces without starts, make sure the team has enough time and motivation to build the boat speed up to the required intensity. As I have mentioned before, high-intensity pieces without starts tend to be a bit softer than desired so attention has to be paid to the buildup for these pieces. In practice, take opportunities to paddle in different wind and water conditions. Also, remember to hone the skills of the drummer and steersperson as well as the

paddlers. How effective is the steering? How effective are the calls used by the drummer and steersperson? Are they lining the boat up effectively for starts? Do the paddlers, steersperson, drummer, and coach use the same language?

Cool-Down

When the workout is done, congratulate the team, summarize the learning and use this as a chance to get some fun into the workout: a start, a drill, a joke. For a cool-down, have the team paddle easy for about 10 minutes, and make sure the last bit of this, at least, is with their best technique.

Technical Plan

There are many different ways to paddle a dragon boat. A coach's technical plan is his or her chosen technical ideal and the means by which they intend to advance their team toward this ideal. Coaches cannot effectively proceed with coaching technique without having a

Photograph by Jens Ronneberger

Coaches, like Chris Edwards of the Outer Harbour Senior Women, take a moment to motivate and focus their crews before they leave the dock and head to the start line.

clear picture of the stroke they are wishing to achieve. For recreational teams, the technical plan can be simple. The most successful recreational teams are those where everyone does the same thing at the same time, and has a good time doing it. Defining the style for your team in a clear, simple way that the paddlers understand is crucial to attaining this cohesion. Dragon boat technique is addressed elsewhere in this book. My contribution to this topic is only to clearly state that both coach and paddler must to be attentive to this facet of training as I believe it to be the most important determiner in team success. Many courses are available to both coaches and paddlers to learn different views of stroke styles and mechanics.

RACE DAY PLANS

≠ ≠

An actual race is only a small part of a race day. Paddlers need to have food, fluids, warm-up times, staging time, race times, and uniforms, among other things, to make sure race days run as seamlessly as possible so full attention can be directed to actually racing. Paddlers, coaches or managers can take care of these details.

RACE PLANS

≠ ≠

Warm-Up

For most regattas, on-water warm-up time is limited to around seven minutes. As this is a very short time, a comprehensive dry land warm-up must be done, as addressed earlier. On the water, the team must paddle with some intensity and discipline immediately. My suggestion for the warm-up is to integrate some segment paddling, some race-pace paddling, and a start leading into race pace (at least

20 seconds) in the first five minutes of the warm-up. This will give the paddlers some physical, technical, and pacing work before the race. I suggest aiming to leave a couple minutes between your last intense piece and the start of the race for the paddlers to recover and focus on the race. This is usually taken care of by the procedure used to line up the crews for the race.

Being on the Start Line

Paddlers must focus on only the race at the start line. Specifically, only the first couple strokes of the race. Reminders from the drummer, steersperson or teammates to relax, focus and breathe are often productive. In addition, the paddlers must listen carefully and respond immediately to requests from the drummer or steersperson to position the boat. Great discipline is required. Lining up for a race should be practised regularly before race day to hone the paddling and mental skills required.

The Race Plan

Race plans need to be rehearsed over and over in practice to be executed as flawlessly as possible on race day.

Photograph by Jens Ronneberger

This team meets in a quiet spot at the 2006 Club Crew Championships in Toronto, Ontario, to review the race plan and to receive some last-minute motivation and inspiration from the coach.

Everyone must understand the objectives of each part of the race, each call and where their focus should be. The most important race strategy is to have a plan before going on the water for the race and to stick to it!

I would suggest going into every regatta with a plan that is practised and understood, and fine-tune it between races. Be careful not to reinvent your plan on race day because of what is seen in another team. Your plan must be specific to the strengths of your own team. In the pre-race pep talk, specific facets of the plan can be reviewed and highlighted. Some teams use group mental imagery before a race and go through the entire race in their minds. Post-race, the team should meet with the coach to review how the race went, congratulate and acknowledge what went well, and make a plan for improvement in the next race.

There is a huge psychological component to

The "race ready" position at the start line has all paddles buried fully or partially, depending on the wind and water conditions. A held start at the Montreal Olympic Basin ensures a fair lineup of six boats before the start horn is sounded.

effective racing, especially for 500-metre racing as it requires such explosive intensity and technical integrity, and leads to such physical discomfort far before the end of the race. Paddlers must possess both calm focus and extreme drive. There are many fabulous books that address mental training and I will not do so here.[2]

Although dragon boats race in a variety of distances, I will focus my attention on the 500-metre distance, the most common one. For this distance, in my opinion, the best race plan is one that aims to reach the team's maximum 500-metre pace right after the start and has calls made to maintain that speed. For example, calls like "power 10 now" for 10 hard strokes should be directed at helping boat speed stay consistent rather than actually increasing speed, unless a slow pace was accidentally set in a race. Pace

changes in response to calls throughout a race require extreme unity and discipline to be effective and, more often than not, are more a reflection of the original pace being too slow than any great skill on the part of the team.

Starts

But first, a crew must get off the line. The generally accepted dragon boat start is to do about six strokes deep and hard and then about 16 fast and short (I will call this the over-rate) before extending stroke length to race pace. The idea is to first lift and move the boat forward and then to get the boat moving faster than race pace. Lifting a still boat and moving it forward requires the paddlers to have solid strokes

Photograph by Jens Ronneberger

Photograph by Jens Ronneberger

Paddlers, still focusing on good technique, "empty the tank" at the finish in an attempt to be first across the line. Many races are won or lost in this final portion.

with some decent length and have the focus on moving the boat, rather than moving the paddles. Deep clean strokes will move the boat forward while creating clean water for paddlers further back in the boat to do the same. As the boat starts to move, the stroke rate and/or stroke length must increase to keep the boat accelerating. Some crews will start with shorter strokes and increase stroke length as the boat starts to move (1/2, 3/4, full for the first three strokes, for example). Others, and my preference, will keep close to full stroke length and increase stroke rate. My opinion is that crews, from novice to advanced, are strong enough to move the boat with a full stroke on the first couple strokes if they are dynamic strokes. Increasing the stroke rate through these initial strokes will lead to a smoother and more effective increase in boat speed and transition to the over-rate. For the over-rate, although the rate is high, paddlers must focus on keeping the strokes deep and moving the boat forward to avoid the common folly of spinning the paddles quickly without the accompanied boat speed. Remember, first and foremost, the goal is to move the boat forward fast, not move the paddles fast.

With 100 metres left, there's really no thinking, it's just endurance and just focusing on the pain and trying to ignore the pain at the same time, which is a strange thing. You've got to focus on where the pain is and try to eliminate the feeling of fatigue and really just focus on maximizing each stroke, which is a difficult thing when everything's on fire.

As far as the pain goes, you've got an immediate choice as soon as that feeling sets in: Do I choose to keep pushing it or do I choose to relent and give in to my body's reaction to working too hard?

The test of an endurance athlete is to push that limit and push that boundary and tell the body it's got to sit tight for a couple of minutes as you see how much you can do.

Any good endurance athlete will say that maintaining their form and their technique through those moments of pain and fatigue is probably the most key aspect to maintaining the speed. It's really easy to break down the technique and not be as snappy to return to the setup phase in the kayak stroke.

— Adam van Koeverden, Oakville, Ontario, Toronto Star, August 21, 2008. Van Koeverden is the Silver Medallist in the 2008 Olympics men's K-1, 500 metres. Van Koeverden took time to speak to dragon boaters at a 2008 spring training camp in Florida.

I have found that novice teams can get too complicated with their starts. For example, if a newer team that has not yet developed a long working stroke decides to do a 1/2, 3/4, full start for the first three strokes, the half stroke is so short it barely moves the boat. I have been coaching some breast cancer survivor teams and have yet to find a team that cannot muscle through a near-full length first stroke, starting with blades fully buried. The other trap for novice teams is an overemphasis on a fast over-rate stroke. Coaches of novice crews should make sure their start procedure is most effective for their crew, and for some, this involves removing the over-rate altogether.

A dragon boat is a big heavy boat that takes a lot to accelerate and a lot to decelerate. For this reason, crews must be aggressive and technical on their start to get the boat going as effectively as possible. When it comes to the finish, the strong momentum in this boat does us a favour as the boat will not decelerate as quickly because of fatigue as a lighter boat.

Finishes

For a finish, the idea is to use up any remaining energy in a technically sound way to reach the finish line as quickly as possible. Depending on the crew's pacing, this will either result in an increase in speed or, more likely, limit the decrease in pace that comes with fatigue. A crew that accelerates considerably for the finish most likely paced too conservatively earlier in the race and could improve overall performance by aiming for a higher overall pace or a more aggressive start. For most teams, maintaining focus on keeping technique consistent on the finish will be required as tired paddlers easily shorten up and become less technically efficient. Some crews will actively increase the stroke rate for the finish. The effectiveness of this should be measured beforehand as it can give a false sense of increased boat speed.

Transitions

As a coach, I dedicate a lot of time toward fine-tuning transitions. By transitions, I mean the parts of the race where, for a couple of strokes, the focus is on a shift in stroke rate or rhythm. Some possible transitions are: deep start strokes to over-rate, over-rate to race pace, race pace to finish. These times are crucial as a lack of focus and practice can result in a change that should take a couple strokes taking more or not happening effectively at all. Why I find transitions so important is that, if teams can execute their transitions effectively every time, they can gain valuable distance on their competitors at no energetic cost. And, in the case of the transition to race pace, race pace is found easiest immediately. If race pace is not found on the transition, it is difficult to move the team toward it during the body of the race. The most important requirement in executing these transitions is all paddlers understanding what they are required to change in their stroke to accomplish it. For example, crews that have been emphasizing the blade entry and front of the stroke during the over-rate need to focus on pulling through the back of the stroke at their transition to race pace.

Photograph by Barry Wojciechowski

It's not all about the bling, but medals are a tangible reminder of success. At the Thunder Bay festival in Ontario, the medals await the awards ceremony.

CONCLUSION
≠ ≠

There is so much that can be covered on the topic of dragon boat coaching. This chapter is merely a taste. The vast amount of detail that can be applied to coaching can be overwhelming and not necessary for a novice coach or recreational team. Ultimately, what is most important is for the team to have goals and a mandate, and a coach to provide the structure to facilitate meeting the objectives defined in these. As a team, a paddler, or a coach gets more advanced, so too do the tools applied to coaching. In other words, coaches, like the paddlers they coach, must build their skills gradually, layer upon layer, until they reach the level that they wish to accomplish. To do this, there are many resources available to build on what has been presented here and I encourage you to explore these.

Photograph by Heather Maclaren

Women on Water (WOW) from Fort Langley, British Columbia, at the Bill Ailey Memorial Regatta in Burnaby, British Columbia.

NOTES

1. The "Calgary Dragons" is a fictional team, the name chosen as a tribute to my hometown.

2. **Editor's Note:** For suggested books, see "Additional Reading" in this book.

6

龙 Teams and
Teamwork 船

Andrew Fox

Photograph by Heather Maclaren

The False Creek Mixed Team shows its form during the 2,000-metre "Guts and Glory" race in Vancouver, British Columbia.

Teams and teamwork — here is the real backbone of dragon boat as a whole. Is it a sport, a recreational activity, or a hobby? Do not ask any self-respecting dragon boater that question. Dragon boat competitors are some of the most passionate people on the planet when it comes to their sport. Co-workers and family members often ask about their "rowing"; a standard answer is always spoken. "It's paddling, not rowing. It's going great, thanks for asking."

From here it all starts. What kind of team are we — try it once, weekly recreational, increasingly competitive, very competitive, highly competitive, elite, and, finally, a national team? Each of these has a certain team composition, a group dynamic, a distinct

My personal experience started years ago, when I watched my first dragon boat race in the pouring rain. Everyone was soaked to the skin; the outside temperature was cold; and, the competition on the water was intense. Despite all of these factors, the support these paddlers gave to each other and their competing team members made me aware that was the sport for me.
— Deborah Woodbeck, Winnipeg, Manitoba

team makeup, an on-the-water manner, a certain feel or method in the boat, and its own brand of loyalty and teamwork.

Yet all teams at every stage of the sport bring to bear the same intensity and enthusiasm at their own level of competition. This is what makes dragon boating great. All teams are welcomed into the fold and offered an opportunity to play or compete with other teams that are like-minded. Some want to rip and burn it up. Others want to execute well and participate equally. Many want to be with friends and have some fun on the water.

The makeup of teams is as unique and diverse as mankind itself, so how is it that teams have similar dynamics and characteristics, and how do these play out in the sport of dragon boat racing?

RECREATIONAL TEAMS

Let's start with a recreational team. Generally, it is made up of boyfriends and girlfriends, a few guys from work, a girl who just joined the company, and a guy who used to paddle when he was younger. Now somebody gets the idea that, for charity, "we should raise some money and try dragon boating" … so they do so.

This recreational team generally practises a few times in advance of an event. A group of 18 to 20 people cobble together and come out for a practice or two. Some help is found from a "fit neighbour" of the organizer to fill out the boat on race day. Also, one of the crew members has a sister who is really small but can yell like she has for a horn for a voice, so she is the perfect drummer.

The team rents a steersperson on race day and goes down the course like it is the Stanley Cup final. At the end of the race, all the group wants to know is: if anyone fell in; "did we beat that other team

Photograph by Heather Maclaren

A team celebrates the end of a race at the 2008 False Creek Women's Regatta in Vancouver, British Columbia.

that was also raising some money"; and, "where's the BBQ." They really don't care about their time (unless they did it last year), and they all hope it does not rain.

From that team, you will get three people who are hooked. They leave the safe haven of this friendship-driven crew and venture off to find a more competitive one. They meet up with a small group of people they may have seen at an event or

two. They are looking to "bulk up" with a few new bodies to take on that team that seems to beat them every time out.

Here a transformation takes place and a recreational team becomes a crew. This crew wants to improve, enjoy the sport, have some get-togethers, and race. Often the group is linked by community, friends, family, or work. They are like-minded in terms of their desire to paddle together and practise

Photograph by Ben Lee

Since 1998, the False Creek Women's Regatta has grown from a few entries to over 50 teams from the Lower Mainland, Vancouver Island, and the northwestern U.S. The emphasis is on camaraderie and celebrating the joy of women's dragon boat.

a certain number of times per week. In this team dynamic, the leaders tend to be slightly more eager or experienced and they pull everything together, from rosters to practice times to a coach. The team makeup starts to change as the team really does care how well they race, and rivalries are born. Now the race is on to improve within the confines of the weekly practice schedule.

As for the in-boat crew setup, there tends to be an established and accepted position for all. The lineup is the same as last year's. Paddlers have their favourite seats and partners. They get in the boat, based on who has been on the team longer, or the role they have in the sponsoring company. Life is typically good as the hierarchy is set in advance and everybody knows the score. The coach barks out the

Photograph by Barry Wojciechowski

The front six and engine room give it their all at the Thunder Bay festival in Ontario.

marching orders and the workouts begin.

At season's end, a few feathers have been undoubtedly ruffled, with the "up and comers" wanting some changes, others wanting fewer. Someone is starting a family, and two others are changing jobs or moving away. Once again, the recruiting drive ramps up, and the top players are enticed away to a team that owns their own paddles and life jackets, and that came second last year.

COMPETITIVE TEAMS
≠ ≠

In this increasingly competitive team, the dynamics of the crew start to unfold based on where one sits in the boat. The race strategy is broken down and an assignment, based on seating rows, is given to each section of the boat. The front six are the first three rows, often called the pacers. The next four rows consist of eight paddlers who are dubbed the engine room. And

Photograph by William Ng

A tight race unfolds as three boats try to gain the advantage during the Victoria Dragon Boat Festival in British Columbia.

the final six paddlers are the back six or rockets.

Regardless of the race plan or strategy, most competitive crews use this model in some form or another. In practice, the groups work on stroke technique, tempo, power, and paddling style, based on the position of the paddlers in these three groupings.

In a race, the three sub-groups work together to offer support and take leadership roles at different times as they work down the course. The front six follow the two strokes seated in row one and try not to let the middle eight push the stroke rate too high. All the while, the back six (rockets) try to give a shot of power to the crew when the steersperson or drummer yells for it.

The front, middle, and back exist in all competitive teams, right up to, and including, the national team level crews. Their roles and purposes are similar, yet how they go about their business is

> Having the opportunity to line up at the start line with my fellow team members alongside other boats and waiting for the start to be called is such a fantastic feeling. The only feeling greater than that is paddling your hardest as the boat surges past the finish line.
> — Noel Wong, University of Toronto

the real difference. The battle within the boat rages to this day as all sections claim supremacy and a stake in their crew's successes.

The game plan for the competitive team varies according to different situations. It is affected by the crew members, competition within the race, and the level of experience of the paddlers. If the team races well, the crew members have generally applied the plan and stayed within their ability to deliver the best possible outcome, given the competition that they are up against.

With the season come some wins and losses, some good races, and some, better forgotten. The team tries to adjust its strategy based on the results. As the season ends, there is some turnover and a few former crew members may return. A meeting is held and the group decides to step it up. The highly competitive team is spawned.

In the highly competitive crew, paddling successes, who you paddled with, testing results, and athletic résumés become your ticket to join. The coach or team members recruit paddlers who expect to earn their seats on the boat as others have already done. There are still common threads of friendships stemming from paddling and business relationships, or working out at the gym. You have been invited to be on the team. Remember that talent attracts talent and success is a magnet.

The focus of these crews shifts to the athletes, their paddling skill, physical fitness, and body type. All good crews have a blend of small, medium, and larger athletes to fill the various roles within the crew. As the coach assesses the talent and the crew starts to take shape, hard decisions must be made. The highly competitive team now has to tell a few of its members to retire since there are no seats for them in the competitive boat. Additionally, two or three experienced paddlers want to join since the level of competitiveness has increased. For every person who leaves, there is another paddler looking for that higher competitive challenge.

On the boat of the highly competitive crew, there still exist the three sections of the crew: front, middle, and back. Now their functions become specialized to maximize their value and contribute to the most efficient race plan.

The front six are no longer two strokes and the four controlling the pace. They become a unit of six

Photograph by William Ng

The drummer calls out encouragement and boat commands to her crew at the Victoria Dragon Boat Festival in British Columbia.

paddlers who work together to deliver the pace as outlined in the team's pre-race strategy. They think about the tempo of the stroke and the implementation of planned moves that the crew intends to apply. These could include a series of power strokes to gain an advantage, a faster start to put pressure on another crew, a controlled effort to conserve energy, or any of the many other race strategies that can be used by a highly competitive crew.

The middle eight are still the engine room with responsibility for the thrust of the boat and the guts of any strategic move. These eight generally feel the stroke rate set by the front six, accept it, work with it, or collectively change the rate to suit their mindset. These moves can be good or disastrous.

The back six provide support for the efforts of the two groups ahead of them. This often forgotten back section works hard to establish themselves as valued

Photograph by Jan Oakley

The steersperson keeps the boat on a straight line with the steering oar and positions his body to keep the boat dynamic.

crew members, not just the others in the back. Their role is to react to the steersperson's commands first and offer a boost to the fatiguing middle eight and pacers up front.

In the end, the team has its share of issues as paddlers gain more race experience. They form their own ideas of the race strategy and the desired stroke rate. Further, there are more opinions of who should be in the boat and where.

In the more competitive crews, drummers and steerspersons become as much a part of the crew as any paddler, and, in many cases, more irreplaceable. Crews do not want to go out without their own drummers and steerspersons.

Top quality drummers are no longer hood ornaments that are light on the drum seat and big of voice. They (95 percent female) must understand the race strategy and get their crews to follow it. A constant barrage of encouragement does not cut it anymore. What is needed is the ability to instill confidence in the crew, make honest assessments of where the crew is in the race, and assess what has worked and what must change. This is where these diminutive crew members are worth twice their weight in gold.

Steerspersons (95 percent male) must have a solid command of their crew's attention and respect to be successful. The crew must be confident in the person at the helm. Steerspersons must be forceful, aware, and responsive to what is happening in the race. The knowledge of their crew's strengths and weaknesses, coupled with a knowledge of the course and the surrounding competitors, are used to make the needed moves or changes to the race plan to get the best results. Again, top quality steerspersons are worth their weight in gold.

Many high-level crews have a set strategy going into a race. They plan on when they will make a move, what the stroke rate will be, and when they will ramp up to finish the race. The highest-level crews will adjust these as the race unfolds and/or when the positioning in the regatta allows for a second-place finish or a preferred lane draw based on time or placement. Surprising to many, the highest level crews do not try and set their fastest times at each outing. Herein arises an elite crew.

ELITE TEAMS
≠ ≠

Elite crews take for granted all the race elements that the increasingly competitive and the highly competitive crews strive to deliver. They believe that they can win every race, distance, heat, event, and gold medal. This does not mean that they do or will. But they have the unwavering belief and desire to do it, and the training to back it up. Elite crews deliver consistently. They produce quality efforts and turn in fast times without fail. The differences between the best of the best become smaller and smaller.

The three groups on the crew work together, supporting each other's efforts. The front six become the stroke. No longer does this responsibility fall on one person; the group is the stroke. Yes, there is a lead, but this person is not alone, rather a part of the group.

The middle engine paddlers, who pride themselves on their physicality, still provide the power and brawn as their bodies are generally bigger. But they know that they must deliver a rate that the front six can translate into an effective running pace for the crew.

On the elite crews, the back six consists of a group of aware and savvy racers with the strength

Photograph by Normand Beaulieu

Teams racing at the highest levels train year-round to ensure success. Members of the Canadian Senior Women Crew show their brawn at the 2007 World Dragon Boat Racing Championships in Sydney, Australia.

and ability to boost their crewmates when needed. They often start or engage the moves that spark a push by the crew.

Elite-style crews have the same issues as any group of people or athletes with respect to personal relationships and varying thoughts on what will work best. However, these are laid to rest before the race and a single race plan is engaged and implemented. This is why the best of the best always seem to deliver regardless of wave conditions, lane depth and width, other competitors' strategies, and the many other factors that make dragon boat racing unpredictable and exciting.

Finally elite crews do not always try to race their fastest race, all the time, in every heat. They use all

their members; they know the competition; they deliver quality; and they conserve where they can. Elite crews look at the bigger picture, at the event as a whole, and strategize accordingly.

NATIONAL TEAMS
≠ ≠

From the elite teams is built the core of many national crews. There are numerous models and success stories describing how these are applied by

The Canadian Senior Open Crew delivers on the finish at the 2007 World Dragon Boat Racing Championships in Sydney, Australia.

various programs. National-level crews represent the best of the best, groups of individuals with an ingrained sense of competition and drive. The best-in-the-world mindset is part of their makeup.

In the boat, these competitors are quick to respond to the feel of the boat. They can tell if something is needed, be it stroke rate, power, lift, or surge. At the national level, the three groups' boundaries become more blurred. All the paddlers understand the roles of the others and see themselves as part of the whole. National-level paddlers are not only the best in that seat, they also make the person beside, in front, and behind them better. The sum total of the crew is greater then the sum of its parts.

National crews use different lineups, based on the race, type of boat, weather conditions, water depth, and the overall feel of the crew setup. The

Photograph by Jan Oakley

The strokes of the Canadian Senior Women's Crew show their precision form at the 2007 World Dragon Boat Racing Championships in Sydney, Australia.

crew dynamics are also slightly different at this level. Each crew member wants to be the best person for that seat. Not the best available, but the best. Paddlers embrace a change of seats if more speed can be found. Many adjust the length of their paddles, depending on race distance and their seat position. True competitors at the national level invite a challenge from their crewmates and earn the seat and respect, based on ability, attitude, and the buy-in to the process of the team winning regardless of who is placed in the boat. A tag line that could be used is "one win–all win." But do not believe for one minute that national-level paddlers want to sit out for the betterment of their teams. They do it, but this cuts them to the bone to watch their crewmates go to battle without them.

Photograph by Jan Oakley

The technique shown by the Canadian Senior Open Crew, racing at the 2007 World Dragon Boat Racing Championships in Sydney, Australia, is a reflection of the crew's experience and training.

CONCLUSION

This summary of the various crew types and levels is only the tip of the dragon's nose. The world of dragon boating is all-encompassing with groups of people coming together at different levels, and participating and competing in the great sport of dragon boat racing. The complexities of crews and people are vast.

To foster teamwork and develop a program that is successful, all those involved need to understand where their crew or club stands. What are the goals and objectives? If a short-, medium- and long-term plan is developed, the likelihood of a happy and healthy group increases.

Being on the water in a small craft with 19 other women is an amazing experience. We decide, as a team, what our objectives are, and we commit as individuals to strengthen our bodies in order to achieve our goals …

— Joan Hunter, Toronto

Cascades Grand Masters of Chelsea, Quebec, do a high five and congratulate their competitors after winning a hard-fought race.

Photograph by Jan Oakley

The development of a crew should not be based only on the desire to move up the dragon boat racing food chain and compete at the highest possible level. The team should consider the boundaries within which it is working and make decisions based on its members and the prospect of attracting new ones.

As some programs grow in membership, the "A-team" and "B-team" concepts are introduced. In this model, the A-team grabs the best paddlers and the B-team is the feeder team. This structure has worked with varying degrees of success. Not all B-team members want to be on the A-team, and not all A-team members will take kindly to being "demoted" to the B-team. Hence, a note of caution and some preparation need to be made before a club takes that leap into expansion. It can be a slippery slope. However, managed well, with care and attention to the needs and desires of both crews and each paddler, the model of two teams can bring a world of riches to a club. Team members gain the ability to train together; cross-pollinate skills; practise with a full boat; participate in a developmental program; and grow within the club. The club benefits from the economies of scale offered by a wider membership base.

The measurement of a good dragon boat program is not calculated by the number of medals or wins; it is a reflection of the effect of the many ... a contribution to the community and sport of dragon boating. Without your rivals, there is no race, no reward, no challenge, no fun.

I encourage all of you to contribute to your clubs, learn from the worthy, discard the meaningless, and contribute to the solution.

7

Voice of the Beast

龙　　　　　　　　　　　　　船

Albert McDonald

The *Beasts Blog* is a regular feature that is posted on the Dragon Boat East website[1] but is not archived. The opinions expressed are those of Albert McDonald and not necessarily those of Dragon Boat East. Three *Beasts Blog* entries follow.

"We're in the Same Boat," *Beasts Blog*, May 19, 2008
≠ ≠

In most situations in life "being in the same boat" means that two or more people are facing the same challenge together. In dragon boat paddling, 22 people literally are "in the same boat." It should be a simple proposition: 22 people of different physical size, offering different skills, trying to move a boat down the water faster than the other groups of 22.

Sometimes though, we make it complicated. This happens when people try to assign more or less value to their contribution in the boat. I don't know why people do this. I suspect the reason is that successful people in general like to be measured, and because, invariably, crew selection is based on some sort of ranking of individual skills.

There really are not a lot of ways we can differentiate ourselves in a dragon boat, so people invariably use their position in the boat to measure contribution. This happens most often with crews that are just beginning to become competitive. In general they have learned to assign more value to positions nearer the front, as opposed to those in the back, because new people start at the back so they can learn and not interfere with more experienced paddlers in the front. Problems occur once no one is a beginner, and the coach aligns sizes and skills to positions to optimize boat speed. Initially, the coach will encounter resistance from paddlers who think the coach is valuing them less since they are now being put in the back where "the new people" used to be.

This cannot be further from the truth. Ask any established coach, where, all things being equal, their best athletes are, and they will say, "in the back." Look at the boat this way — the front three on each side set tempo and "pull" the boat because the water isn't stirred up and more of the physical structure of the boat is behind them. The back three on each side "push the boat" because most of the physical structure of the boat is ahead of them. This is more difficult because the water is "stirred up" and moving, so the back three must have the skill and the athletic ability to "push" the boat and affect boat speed by generating effective paddle speed and connection in moving water. The middle four are generally larger paddlers (because the boat is wider) and are usually physically stronger, but they do not need the skill to set tempo in dead water or to generate paddle connection in fast-moving water to the degree that the front six or back six do. If anything, the more skilled "engines" would be in seats six and seven, and the better "tempo" paddlers would be in four and five — but many times balancing the boat, from bow to stern, overrides those considerations.

So where you are in the boat is going to depend on your height, weight, temperament, skill, ability to set tempo, ability to find water connection, and the your ability to motivate people and be motivated by people around you. Don't make the mistake of trying to assign "value" to your position. Many dragon boat races are decided by inches, every position is important, and the ability of the coach to match skill sets to the correct position is vital.

Or, put another way, as one of my teammates on the Canadian dragon boat team once told me, "I have no ego when it comes to dragon boat. None. I just want my boat to come first and I want to be in it."

"Train Like the Best," Beasts Blog, April 25, 2008

≠ ≠

Many people want to emulate the best in their sport of choice. That's why Michael Jordan sold sneakers and Tiger Woods sells golf equipment. People buy clothes and equipment to look like the best. They pay for coaching and lessons in an attempt to imitate the best. Sometimes they even hire personal trainers and nutritionists. But what is it like to be on teams with truly great athletes? How do they train? How do they interact with other athletes? This is particularly germane in a team sport like dragon boat, where the performance of the crew is determined solely by the combined contribution of the crew members.

I have competed in various sports for 40 years, and coached for close to 30. In that time, I was lucky enough to train with two truly gifted individuals, track athlete Robert Englehutt and canoer Steve Giles. I have been associated with many, many other excellent athletes, who shared many attributes with Robert and Steve, but no one else that I observed first-hand compared to these two. I believe that Robert and Steve possessed the qualities you would see in the most successful of athletes and achievers in any discipline.

Robert Englehutt is now a highly successful coach of track athletes in Nova Scotia. In 1976, following a comeback from a serious car accident, he ran 3:52 in the 1,500 metres and 8:23 in the 3,000 metres as a high school senior. His hand-timed, provincial high school 1,500-metre record has stood for 32 years. He went on to a highly successful career in distance running, notably in cross-country and marathon competitions. He placed fourth in the 1984 Olympic Marathon trials, in two hours, 16 minutes, and 50 seconds, which was an Olympic qualifying time and still stands as the Nova Scotia provincial record. He competed internationally for Canada in the early to mid-80s.

Steve Giles is a four-time Olympian in sprint canoe singles. He won the 1998 1,000-metre world championship. He won a bronze medal in the 1,000-metre canoe singles event in the 2000 Olympic Games in Sydney, Australia.

Robert and Steve both shared these qualities in their training, as teammates and as competitors. They were as focused on the success of their training groups as they were on themselves. They both understood that they could not do it alone. They both used training partners to measure themselves daily in workouts, and they were ruthless, but in return they were extremely supportive of teammates' efforts. I cannot remember Robert being behind in an interval (over 200 metres, sorry, Robert, but you got no speed), ever, in any workout. He had an unbelievable focus in training. In our canoe group, Steve told me, a very strong runner for a canoer, that if he ever beat me in a running interval — any running interval, ever — I was out of the training group. This led to some very high-intensity running between us, and I'm glad to say I never got kicked out. But I'll also say that I knew that Steve was dead serious. The same guy who was so supportive and would do anything to help me in training would absolutely have kicked me out of the group if he beat me in an interval. Robert and Steve would do anything to help anyone in their training group, and then expect their training partners to train as they did.

They both never acted like they were any better than anyone else in the group. They were confident but humble. You hear this time and again, about successful people. Their will to succeed burns deep inside.

They were slaves to the training program: "10 sets" means "10 sets." The pace time is the pace time. In fact, I've seen both of them get annoyed over the exact same thing (14 years apart). They would get annoyed when people in the group were going FASTER than the set pace. I distinctly remember doing a workout with our track team; it was 20 times 200 metres in 30 seconds, jog back to the start rest. We were easily doing 30s and started going 29 and

28. Robert got annoyed and explained that 20 times 30 meant just that and if we could go faster then we should finish the workout, talk to the coach, and do 29s next time. Of course, come the 18th, 19th, and 20th 200, when Robert was still gliding through 30s and we were fighting to do 34s and 35s, we understood. Steve was exactly the same way. Do the workout, do it well, and don't adjust in the middle.

They both took time to rest, and to let injuries heal. They trained hard but they would not overtrain. If they showed up to practise, it was game on. If they couldn't go 100 percent, they took care of the problem and showed up when they were ready to go. Neither man let the performance of competitors affect their training, racing, or attitude. They both were quiet at training sessions and socially, but when they talked they said a lot in a few words.

When justified, they both would let certain teammates know exactly what they thought, particularly if that teammate committed the crime of being late, not working hard enough, or, especially, being arrogant — anything that affected the quality of the training, or upset a teammate. They would not tolerate bullying or vindictive behaviour against a member of their training group. They did not leave behavioural issues to the coaches; they led by example, and then spoke up when necessary. They understood that an athlete's training group is a reflection of the leaders of the group and they took that role seriously.

Sometimes the focus was too much for an average athlete like me. I laugh when I hear people say that Steve didn't do that much volume or train that hard (in later years, he did lower volume but maintained high intensity). I can remember one cold, windy, rainy day in November 1991 (the fall before the first of Steve's four Olympics), when we did a 16-kilometre session of hard intervals in the morning, at the end of a particularly hard week. It was a Saturday morning, and that afternoon and all day Sunday were scheduled for much-needed recovery. It was raining, it was cold, and it was windy. The workout was a waste of time; everyone was just surviving and going through the motions. At the end of the workout, Steve just quietly informed our coach that he thought we should do the workout again, that afternoon (in even worse weather). I could not believe it, I couldn't understand what possible thought process was behind this. I think I do now.

Be humble, worry about your own improvement, compete hard in practice, always support your teammates and training partners, strive for excellence for the amount of time you have allocated to training, and be a really, really good friend to the average lumberjacks like me on your team or in your training group.

Strive to be better. Train like the best.

"BE COACHABLE," BEASTS BLOG, MAY 6TH, 2008

≠ ⅄

Over the past three years, I have instructed a number of dragon boat coaches at Dragon Boat Canada coaching courses throughout North America. I have been impressed not only by the personal qualities of these individuals, but also by their genuine concern that they are offering the best possible experience for their athletes. Invariably, discussions at these clinics turn to anecdotes about specific experiences these (almost always) volunteer coaches have in the course of a season. In general most coaches have encountered:

- Criticism about crew selection and the feeling that no matter who they put in the boat they will receive negative feedback and, in some cases, personal attacks;
- Second guessing about technical components, such as stroke rate, placement of crew members, stroke mechanics, and general undermining of the coach, particularly if they are female;
- Interference from "team captains" and board members;

- Huge volumes of emails about items of small consequence.

I can tell you that, at its absolute best, coaching dragon boat is not as fun as paddling dragon boat and that, because of the layers of personal dynamics generated by 20 people, it consumes you. Before you criticize your coach, particularly to fellow team members (this is most destructive to team dynamics and almost always gets back to the coach third hand), consider the effort and sacrifice your coach is making on your behalf. Dragon boat is a team sport and, as such, there will be many times that what is best for the team is not 100 percent what is best for you.

My experience has been that the best athletes are, by far, the easiest to coach. Max Tracy, one of our most talented "Dragon Beasts," never offers anything but suggestions that are either positive or constructive in nature. I once went to sit Max in a race in Ottawa, thinking if I rested him in the semi-final, he would be even fresher and stronger in the final and it would enable me to get another rostered spare into a race. Because no one likes to sit, I started to explain this to him. He cut me off and said, "I'll do whatever, don't ever worry about me." It made my life a lot easier — he had no idea about the multiple issues I was dealing with at the time. He then went out and stood in the marshalling area collecting IDs and sweat tops, and supporting his teammates. Your best athletes always put the team first.

Look at yourself before you criticize the coach or say "this isn't the best thing for the team." Maybe it is better for the team — it just isn't better for you. Be coachable. Your team will be benefit.

NOTES

1. **Editor's Note:** *Beast Blogs* are posted on the Dragon Boat East website (*www.dragonboateast. ca*).

8

龙 **The Making of an A-Team** 船

Jim Farintosh

> I get a good workout, have fun, and am constantly learning new things about my stroke and the waters we paddle on. How great is that!
> — Margot Harding, Winnipeg, Manitoba

The challenge of building an A-level team is a marriage of a number of influences, many (but not all) dependent on the coach. For this reason the following comments, while coach-centred, are valuable to all team members.

In simple terms, an A-level result really boils down to establishing a culture of trust, a solid work ethic, and constant attention to all details that encourage excellence. When these things are in place, good athletes come to your program and they stay. With everything in place, quality results are sure to follow.

In dragon boat racing (as in life) it is safe to say that everyone wants to do their best, it's just that some people are willing to make it a higher priority than others, every day. Your job as coach is to help your athletes make that commitment and to be sure they find enough reward in their efforts to continue to grow, year after year. So, how do you do this?

Quality coaching is a partnership with your athletes and this type of relationship is built on a solid foundation of "best practices" that are applied every day. I feel that a listing of some of these key points might be the best way to give an overview to the above task. As you read them, reflect on your own program and see if they

Photograph by Edward Lumb

One of the "winningest" teams on the Canadian dragon boat scene, Toronto-based Mayfair Predators, consistently finishes in the top division.

apply to your team environment. If you can take a few of these ideas and move in the right direction, then you are on your way to developing a better team. I'm sure you can think of others as well, the important thing is that you constantly reflect on your methods, change where necessary and do your best ... your athletes will support you and quickly move "up the alphabet."

PLAN TO WIN
$$\neq \; \not\equiv$$

I am fortunate to have a team in Toronto (the Mayfair Predators) that has had its share of success over the past few years and every time we go to an event, we plan to win. That's not a statement of arrogance,

Photograph by Jan Oakley

Members of the Canadian Senior Open Crew proudly hoist their Canadian flags after singing the National Anthem at the 2007 World Dragon Boat Racing Championships in Sydney, Australia.

that's the way we think. It doesn't always happen, but we are fully prepared to make sure we do everything possible to win every race. The great thing about the Toronto dragon boat community is that there are at least six to eight other teams that think the same way. They are coming to the event to win, not just "do well." This level of competition really keeps everyone honest and nothing less than your best will do. All of our year-round training is set up to get the job done. It takes planning 11 months a year, six days a week. Not everyone wants to put in that kind of time, but welcome to the "A" level.

Photograph by Derek Griffiths

Jim Farintosh and the Mayfair Predators are in a tight race at the 2008 Great White North Dragon Boat Challenge in Toronto, Ontario.

BUILD FLEXIBILITY IN YOUR TEAM

≠ ≭

Crews that consistently perform at the "A" level are able to deal with changing race conditions, personnel issues, travel demands and any number of other stressors that can derail the desired result. Your athletes have to be able to understand that some things are beyond their control and focus on building a positive attitude toward adjusting to the best of their ability to any situation. If they can do this it is a huge advantage, as other aspiring crews may not have this ability. Move people around in the boat, encourage switch hitters, practise in deep water, shallow water, head winds, tail winds, race from behind, race from in front, late finishes, early finishes, every contingency should be practised and mastered. This approach keeps everyone flexible and builds a belief that "whatever happens, we can deal with it." It also keeps things interesting in practice!

WORK AS HARD AS YOUR ATHLETES

≠ ≹

Your personal example shows your team that you are serious about doing well and expect as much from yourself as you do from them. This includes planning, communication, training, sacrifice, and belief in the team. When a team sees a point of leadership that they respect in this regard, you can expect more commitment and constant motivation. Run the hills, make the weight goals, understand what you expect from them, and your example will empower everyone around you.

LAUGH AT YOURSELF A BIT

≠ ≹

A confident athlete is one who can focus, when necessary, and relax at other times. If the coach shows these same attributes, the team feels it has permission to ride emotions "up and down" as it gets ready to break into the A level. Inevitably, the pressure of increased expectations must be confronted. Having a side of your personality that can relax and see a bit of humour once in awhile is an important skill that helps when the team has to turn up the concentration and effort when it really counts.

TRUST MORE, EXPECT MORE

≠ ≹

Eventually, performance is in the hands of the team, and a coach who can help athletes see that they are the ones who have to deal with the "big moment" is making a vital connection. It starts with trust regarding individual training away from the boat, as well as making good decisions around related lifestyle choices. The best program in the world will not get it done if there is little trust on all fronts. Athletes who wake up every day and confirm that trust through their actions can expect more from themselves and their teammates. It's the way A-level teams have to operate.

FIND SOMETHING POSITIVE IN EVERYTHING

≠ ≠

Negative people are rarely successful and, in a team sport, it is doubly true. Trying to get better means risking "failure" every weekend and a diet of negative thoughts can quickly destroy a team's confidence and drive. As a coach I try to make sure that feedback is honest, but always framed around points of progress. What level of team you have doesn't matter. Everyone likes a pat on the back and will accept the areas of need in a much more receptive manner. Stay optimistic and continue to work on getting better, that's the key.

BE FRIENDLY, BUT ACCEPT SOME DISTANCE

≠ ≠

As a coach you wear a number of hats. You have to be a teacher, a motivator, a disciplinarian, an authoritarian, a mentor, a confidant, and, at times, a friend. Coaching is truly a human endeavour and it requires an understanding that you are seen a bit differently by other members of the crew. That difference requires a degree of separation, however hard that might be at times. That distance helps you to remain objective, and to see the best interests of the whole team when tough decisions must be made. Find other circles where you are just "one of the guys," but recognize that more is expected from you on an A-level team. There is too much effort made by too many people for you to see it any other way.

KEEP IN TOUCH

≠ ≠

A team is like a family and everyone needs to know that they are not taken for granted in any way. Some people need more attention, others prefer a bit more privacy, but everyone must know that you as coach are connected with them. Everyone must feel that they have an honest relationship with you on a personal level, and, if there is an issue outside of the boat, that you can be a good listener. This means keeping in touch and making sure that the personal bond is always strong and never taken for granted. A few words of conversation or support at the right time is so important, both ways.

WATCH YOUR WEIGHT
≠ ≠

The journey to becoming an A-level dragon boat athlete can be a long one and it requires patience. It's a good idea to have a few goals that are attained in the short term, as they help the individual feel that they are making progress to becoming the best they can be. One important goal is attaining optimal race weight. Every year in October, I ask my athletes what they believe is their best race weight (their number, not mine) and then we work to make that weight right up to the competition phase of the year. A properly set-up boat with everyone at their ideal weight is a big step forward to the elusive A level. Keep in mind that you as coach are part of that dynamic as well, practise what you preach and others will surely get onboard.

TRAIN LIKE YOU RACE
≠ ≠

As a crew aspires to break into the top ranks, they have to be prepared to race at another level. Lots of crews talk about it, but how many actually challenge themselves to go to that level (both mentally and physically) in practice? Not many. It is important to make people go flat out in very limited doses, perhaps two minutes total of the work volume. Usually I will ask a crew to go a true 100 percent no more than twice in a 75-minute workout. If you are reasonable in your demands, you can expect the crew to collect themselves and give you top effort. Give them time to collect themselves before you start and then go after it. This is stressful, but so is racing. They will become less fearful and set themselves up for new levels of confidence on race day. Then the real fun begins!

Photograph by Jens Ronneberger

Chris Edwards, coach of the Outer Harbour Senior Women, readies his crew for race day in Penang, Malaysia.

THE DEVIL IS IN THE DETAILS

≠ ≠

Top coaches are usually detail-oriented and on race day it pays off in spades. Nothing sets a crew adrift like uncertainty and the more organized you are, the less opportunity for problems to develop on race day. I don't think it is necessary to list the myriad of items that should be clearly communicated beforehand, but the work it takes to lay out details in advance is as important as your race day pep talk. The crew can focus on the task in hand and know that all preparations are in place; all they have to do is perform to the best of their ability. An organized coach is saying to the team, "I'm ready." … and believe me, they will be too.

Photograph by Normand Beaulieu

Each member of the Canadian Grand Dragon Open Crew brings individual strength to a gold medal team at the 2007 World Dragon Boat Racing Championships.

Keep Getting Better Individually and as a Team

$$\neq \not=$$

As a coach you sometimes easily forget that a team is a collection of individuals who need a team dynamic that allows them to clearly see what they have to do as individuals to make the team better. The quality of athletes that pushes a crew into the A level demands (and deserves) a belief that there is interest from the coach in their individual progress, as they generally have the positive ego drive to ensure they will

Photograph by Jan Oakley

The Canadian Senior Mixed Crew members make their way to the award ceremony to collect another gold medal at the 2007 World Dragon Boat Racing Championships.

constantly strive to be better. I often ask my team members to reflect on the questions, "What do I have to do? What do we have to do?" Bottom line, success is a partnership and attention to individual needs shows your team that you respect and value their individual growth as much as the team growth.

SPEND SOME TIME TOGETHER

≠ ≠

Find some time to hang out together, it's an important glue in the fabric of a successful team. It doesn't have to be often or formal, just the occasional chance to relax and see people in another light, outside the boat. Friendships become stronger and when you go to battle, resolve is a little deeper, believe me.

KNOW WHEN TO ACT, WHEN TO IGNORE

≠ ⋡

A team can sometimes be preoccupied with issues not really that important. If the coach reacts to "every little thing," then individuals on the team will start to count on you to be judge and jury all the time. It is important for team members to solve their own problems as much as possible, with the coach only getting involved when absolutely necessary. Save your energy and presence for the important decisions and this practice will allow members to retain ownership of everything else. Team captains can be very helpful in some situations as well.

RESPECT EVERYONE, FEAR NO ONE

≠ ⋡

If your team wants to make the A level, they simply have to see themselves as better than most teams and embrace a belief that they can play with anyone. This requires a confident ego drive and can be seen as being a bit arrogant in some circles, so this attitude has to be balanced with an honest respect for all competitors. After the race is over, make sure they congratulate their competition and they mean it. Without quality competition, there is little value to their efforts. This balance can be difficult to achieve, but will keep everything in perspective as the crew improves. The important lesson of success in competition includes humility. Learn this lesson early.

RACE THE BEST TO GET BETTER

≠ ⋡

If you want to be the best, you have to race the best, plain and simple. Any team that does not take advantage of the opportunities to see how they are progressing against quality competition will rarely make that final step to becoming a contender. It means dealing with defeat initially, but lessons can be learned, adjustments in the race plan made, valuable confidence gained. Otherwise, you're just hoping. Find out which events are being attended by the crews you want to play with and make sure you're there too.

Photograph by Jan Oakley

A commitment to winning is reflected in the faces of the Canadian Senior Open Crew.

LEARN FROM DEFEAT

≠ ≠

As a coach, when your crew loses a race, you must be the consummate salesman. You have to concentrate on learning from the loss and treating it as an opportunity to improve. No crew rises to the top without dealing with defeat … let your crew see that in your actions when this happens. Don't moan about the lane, the boat, the wind conditions. Pull out the positives, concentrate on the things you can control, and focus on a plan to improve. Eventually things will fall in place and it will be your day.

MAKE TOUGH DECISIONS WHEN NECESSARY

≠ ≠

Make no mistake, when you want to build an A-level program, you have to make tough decisions all the time. As coach, you constantly deal with roster decisions, race lineups, chemistry issues, motivation, and a myriad of personal concerns involving passionate and talented people. As stated before, these tasks call upon you to maintain a distance in your personal relationships with crew members. You

I could live comfortably knowing that I may never have to endure another one of those intense practices, as well as the sometimes "painful" administrative aspects of running a team. But I really miss the excitement of racing, and being around the good folks … warriors on the water, who give their last ounce of energy and undivided focus to become "one" tight, synchronized, surging unit; something unique to almost any other activity I have known.

— Dave Battistuzzi, Winnipeg, Manitoba

must face the inevitable tough decisions in a manner that is as objective as possible … and you will make them. Ongoing respect and support from the crew will ensure that you have confidence to do what you need to do, when you need to do it. Be open and transparent in your reasons for your decision. Over time, this is the only way to operate.

KEEP LEARNING AND GROWING
≠ ≢

Every team has its lulls in progress and if team members are not challenged to look at the experience to attain A-level standing as a constant opportunity to learn and grow, you will only get so far as a team. One of the most important tasks I have every year as a coach is to find goals that stretch my team's growth. If properly chosen (and agreed upon by the crew), individuals will get excited about new opportunities and challenges and this ensures that they will return next year with enthusiasm and energy. Personal growth is found through the team journey.

KEEP A CORE GROUP
≠ ≢

When new athletes join a team, they are usually looking for a team environment that says "we want to get better, we will do the work, we will make the commitment in every regard." This culture can be maintained each year by ensuring that a core group understands the ways of the team and can help new members buy into the process. If this is not done, a crew can quickly become sidetracked and lose the single-mindedness that separates the A level from the rest. Consistency in this regard will ensure that the team always has a chance to do well, even with inevitable roster changes year by year.

Photograph by Derek Griffiths

Mayfair Predators race at the 2008 Great White North Dragon Boat Challenge in Toronto, Ontario, on their way to winning gold in the 500-metre A-Division Championship Final.

BUILD A CULTURE OF SUCCESS

≠ ≒

Success breeds success, plain and simple. A good coach will carefully craft season objectives that ensure the crew constantly has a chance to succeed at whatever challenges are put before them. Everyone in the crew has to believe that they will be able to find satisfaction from the efforts of the season, be it improving on the relative standing against their competitors, winning a small regatta or improving average time for the season. Everyone wants to feel some success and, if they do, they will return with increased energy and commitment season after season.

Photograph by Jens Ronneberger

Mayfair Predators win gold at the 2008 Club Crew World Championships in Penang, Malaysia, with a time of 1:58.87 minutes in the 500-metre Premier Mixed Final. Mike Haslam, IDBF (far right), presents the medals.

DON'T BE AFRAID TO WIN
$$\neq \; \neq$$

Get past the fear of winning, some crews are paralyzed at the prospect of breaking through at an important regatta. Top crews believe they will win, every time. They do not waste energy and anxiety on their fears, they focus and perform to the best of their ability and good things happen. Talk to your athletes about the trust in the boat and that the best effort lies in controlling the things they can control and not even considering the rest … it's just not important. When a crew has had an experience where this actually works, they will never look back. They will only look ahead to the next crew they will paddle through on their way to the A level.

Photograph by Edward Lumb

Mayfair Predators celebrate their win at the 2008 Great White North Dragon Boat Challenge in Toronto, Ontario, the culmination of their most successful season ever.

CELEBRATE SUCCESS
≠ ≭

When you make some improvement, make sure your team knows it. Everyone likes (and needs) positive reinforcement and the glow of accomplishment really helps keep people going through the inevitable setbacks on the journey to becoming a better crew. The celebration can be big or small, but giving everyone a chance to enjoy special moments is so important. We all work harder when we feel enjoyment. That's what life is all about!

Summary

For all the points listed here, the really important difference in A-level crews and all the others is the commitment to do the necessary work and the trust shown in the coach and each other. When this is in place, good things happen on a consistent basis. I hope some of the above points open some new directions for your crew management as you aspire to get better.

A final comment. When the racing is all said and done (as far as I am concerned), the only thing you "win," when you attain A-level status, is respect. Respect for other crews, your teammates, and, most important, yourself. Respect is hard-won and easily lost, so as your crew improves, accept the responsibility to carry yourself with dignity and sportsmanship. The A-level reputation is earned both on and off the water.

All the best in your dragon boat endeavours.

9

Common Injuries, Prevention, and Treatment

龙

船

Dr. David Levy

Lots of people have an addiction — drinking, gambling, etc. I'm addicted to paddling and just can't get enough!

— Christine O'Neill, Calgary, Alberta

Dragon boating is a sport that is a lot of fun. It is also a sport that can challenge your aerobic and anaerobic capacity and stress upper body, back, and core strength. All of this plus the psychological benefits of working with a team, forming lifelong friendships and the endorphin high of training, competing, and pushing your personal bar higher. If you let it, dragon boating can be a sport, an exercise routine, an antidepressant, or an empowering addition to your life.

As with any sport, all these physical and emotional advantages do come with the possibility of some detriment to your well-being. Underlying health issues, poor conditioning, faulty technique, or overuse leads to injury and, consequentially, to downtime. How to prevent, recognize, and intervene early are important in minimizing those potential stumbling blocks.

PREVENTION OF INJURY

$$\ne \ne$$

Prevention of injury starts long before you get into the boat. You must recognize the demands of the sport and it is imperative that you be realistic about your physical abilities and limitations, and fitness level. This is not said to dissuade you from undertaking the challenges but to prepare you to face them safely.

Some folks recommend that a preparticipation physical evaluation (PPE) should be a prerequisite for competitive dragon boat athletes of all ages. The primary objectives of a PPE are to provide a structural environment in which to identify and maintain the health and safety of an athlete and to identify illness, injuries, or chronic medical conditions that may endanger the health and safety of athletes and of those with whom they practise and compete.[1]

An objective of the PPE is to screen for conditions that may predispose a competitive athlete to injury or illness. However, there is no literature to support the concept that a PPE will predict who will develop an orthopaedic injury or that it prevents or reduces the severity of an orthopaedic injury in an athlete.[2] In addition, a case series by B.J. Maron and others looked at 158 athletes who died suddenly and noted that the cardiovascular abnormality responsible for death was prospectively identified in only one athlete.[3] The results of such studies are confusing but despite the lack of evidence that PPEs, as they are conducted today, are able to prevent injury or illness, any early recognition and treatment of a problem may minimize time lost from training and competition.

It is probably safe to presume that for most people, physical activity does not pose any undue problem or hazard. However, any individual about to undertake a demanding activity, such as dragon boating, should ask themselves:

- Have you ever had heart trouble or experienced chest pain?
- Have you had periods of feeling faint or dizzy?
- Have you been told that you have high blood pressure?
- Are you on any cardiovascular medication?
- Have you had a bone or joint problem, such as arthritis, that has been aggravated by exercise?
- Do you have any other pre-existing ailment, such as connective tissue or autoimmune disorder, or cancer?
- Have you had major surgery or an organ transplant?
- Are you over 45 and not accustomed to vigorous physical activity?

These would all be reasons to consult your family doctor, a sport medicine physician, or specific specialist before embarking on this strenuous athletic endeavour.[4]

CONDITIONING

Conditioning for dragon boating is of utmost importance, as covered in earlier chapters. It is important to emphasize that the explosive power you need to be a successful racer comes from working on your strength and endurance. Well-toned muscles and aerobic and anaerobic conditioning will give your body its best chance at sporting success and its best defence against injury. Make sure that you train for the challenge. Cross-training and sport specific training are key elements of your preparation as is working on a solid core.

How much endurance and strength you and your teammates have is a pivotal factor in determining whether your team can sustain multiple heats and still have enough left to win when it most counts — in the finals.

INJURIES

In spite of being healthy and well conditioned,

Dragon boating means focus, fitness, friendship. "Focus" means being transformed into a living, breathing, synchronized machine. "Fitness" means a cardio and resistance training routine that is so much fun you forget you are exercising. "Friendship" means smiles and hugs and feeling like I belong.
— Dana Copeland, London, Ontario

there is still a potential for injury in dragon boating. Even with good technique, the constant repetitive strain on the muscles, tendons, and joints can take its toll. The most common injuries are overuse injuries caused by repetitive strain on tissues that leads to mechanical failure and small and large tears in muscles and tendons. The tissue breakdown can happen over a long period, as a result of gradual fatigue in training, or immediately, because a sudden excessive strain as one might experience in the ballistic action of the finishing strokes of a race has occurred. In dragon boating, the target tissues for such strain are the hands and wrists, the shoulders and neck, the mid and lower spine, and their adjacent muscles and tendons.

HAND AND WRIST INJURIES

Repetitive grasping of a paddle for prolonged periods of time with the resistance that one experiences with aggressive strokes, stresses the flexor tendons of the hand and may lead to inflammation. The additional concern with flexor tendonitis is that the increased volume of the inflamed tendon may trigger an associated carpal tunnel syndrome. This occurs in rare cases. Usually, treating the tendonitis with modification of activity, ultrasound, laser, and the use of non-steroidal anti-inflammatory drugs (NSAID), such as aspirin or ibuprofen, is a helpful approach. If this regime is not sufficient to resolve the problem, the use of a resting splint and possibly a corticosteroid injection into the tendon sheath may be considered.

The most common inflammation of the tendon and its synovial membranous covering is de Quervain's tenosynovitis, also known as paddler's wrist. As one cocks the wrist out (extends) and up (abducts) when "reaching" with each stroke, the tendons on the back and outside of the wrist near the thumb, the abductor tendons (pollicus longus and extensor pollicus brevis), become inflamed. Many patients

Photograph by Jan Oakley

The repetitive grasping of the paddle can contribute to injury.

experience difficulty with grasping objects firmly, an effort that can become painful and disabling.

A nice little manoeuvre that you can do to "self-diagnose" this problem is called the Finkelstein Test (see Figure 1). With the affected thumb flexed and held in the palm of your hand by closing your other fingers over it in a fist and then adducting or bending your wrist away from your thumb, still

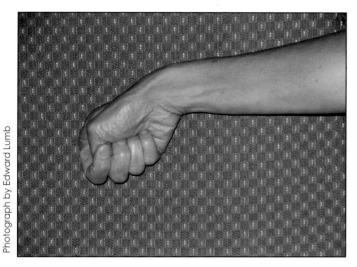

Photograph by Edward Lumb

Figure 1: For the Finkelstein Test, make a fist with your thumb far enough inside the fist to touch the little finger. Move your wrist in the direction of the little finger to stretch the thumb side of your hand. Does it hurt?

studies, gained symptomatic relief from rest and NSAIDs alone.[5]

FOREARM OVERUSE INJURIES

≠ ⩼

keeping a tight grasp over your own thumb and pulling it with the manoeuvre, you will feel pain in the back of the thumb, in the abductor and extensor tendons, extending up your hand and past the crease of your wrist. This would be considered a positive Finkelstein's test for de Quervain's tenosynovitis.

If you have made the diagnosis, see your doctor for confirmation and treatment. Again, modification of activities, local therapeutic modalities, and the judicial use of NSAIDs (topical or oral) may be sufficient to allow the problem to resolve. When the problem is resistant to such treatment, a steroid injection and/or immobilization in a thumb spica splint that does not allow the thumb to extend or flex can be useful. A 2003 study that pooled the results of seven investigations concluded that cortisone alone cured 81 percent of cases, injection and splinting cured 61 percent, and splinting alone cured 14 percent. Interestingly, in spite of attempts at treating these conditions conservatively, *no* patients, in these

The repetitive strain of the "reach" and "catch" of the dragon boat stroke puts excessive recurrent loads on the extensor and flexor muscles, and tendons of the forearm, potentially leading to what is commonly known, in sport vernacular, as tennis elbow and golfer's elbow. Tennis elbow, or lateral epicondylitis, is an overuse syndrome related to excessive wrist extension. For the purist, this condition should be referred to as "extensor tendinopathy." As you "reach," you extend and abduct the wrist. This movement leads to irritation of the extensor carpi radialis brevis tendon, the common wrist extensor, just before its proximal attachment at the lateral elbow (epicondyle). The severity of pain ranges from relatively trivial to an almost incapacitating pain that may keep the patient awake at night. Even everyday activities, such as taking a carton of milk out of the refrigerator or picking up a cup, may be painful. Using a keyboard may become an arduous task.

Photograph by Jan Oakley

Paddlers show full extension as they reach at the front of the paddle stroke.

Treatment, as for most repetitive strain injuries, consists of modifying or avoiding aggravating activities; protecting the healing environment with a counter-pressure forearm brace; decreasing pain with modalities through physiotherapy; breaking down scar tissue and restoring flexibility and strength with manual therapy and acupuncture; and gradually returning to activity. Occasionally, corticosteroid injection is used along with physiotherapy. Surgery may even be required in more resistant cases.

Medial epicondylitis, or golfer's elbow, is caused by repetitive strain of the wrist flexor and pronator muscle and tendon groups and is referred to as "flexor/pronator tendinopathy." As you "catch" and "pull" through the stroke, these forearm muscles control your wrist movements and can eventually pay the price of overuse.

Treatment is the same as that for lateral (extensor)

tendinopathy. In both cases, poor technique can contribute to the severity and recurrence of these injuries. Reviewing stroke mechanics with your coach is advised.

For these conditions, there are other treatment choices that cannot be fully discussed in a short chapter. Suffice it to say that if any one of these options was consistently helpful and had a good evidence base for its successful outcome, it would have been specifically mentioned.

One more point worth mentioning is that elbow pain can often be aggravated, or even caused, by problems with the cervical spine (neck), upper thoracic spine (upper back), and associated neural structures. The twisting that is involved during the "reach," "catch," and "pull" phases of your stroke can put excessive torsion through these structures and aggravate underlying conditions. One's physician must keep this in mind when presented with a dragon boater who has elbow or shoulder pain.

SPINAL PAIN

≠ ⱦ

As alluded to above, underlying spinal problems, such as osteoarthritis of facet joints, degenerative disc disease, or chronic disc herniation in the cervical, thoracic or lumbar (low back) spine, can be exacerbated by the stroke mechanics of dragon boating. These problems, along with irritation of the connective tissues, muscles, tendons, and ligaments, can all be aggravated by faulty stroke technique and by overuse. To prevent these problems, a good back strengthening and core stability program should be part of every paddler's exercise regime. These spinal problems can flare and adversely affect every part of your daily life, so let pain be your guide. Do not ignore the symptoms and simply "soldier on" at the expense of your future health. If symptoms occur, rest, get treatment, and rehabilitate properly with sport specific exercise before returning to this demanding sport.

SHOULDER INJURIES

≠ ⱦ

One could easily write a chapter on shoulder injuries alone. As might be expected in a paddling sport, this structure is the most commonly injured in dragon boating. An injury can occur in almost all aspects of the stroke and even in the weight room.

The shoulder is a ball and socket joint that allows for a great range of movement and an equally great range of problems. Some of the tendons of the rotator cuff, the muscles that move your shoulder, sit in a precarious position between the ball and socket. As you raise your arm up, especially at the "reach" and "finish" of the stroke, these tendons get squeezed or "impinged" between the ball and the structures (bones and ligaments) that make up the socket. This is referred to as impingement syndrome. This impingement can lead to swelling and pain (inflammation) and even to tears in the tendons (supraspinatous, biceps). It can also lead to pinching and swelling of the (subacromial) bursa, a small fluid-filled sack that tries to protect the tendon from getting injured between the bones. This is called subacromial bursitis.

Impingement is a clinical sign of an underlying problem, not a diagnosis. It can be the result of abnormal anatomy of the socket (hooked acromion), arthritis, or bone spurs resulting from degenerative joint disease or disease affecting the rotator cuff. Injury to the nerves that control the muscles about the shoulder can also cause impingement syndrome. However, the most common cause of impingement syndrome and rotator cuff injury is overuse. Repetitive strain fatigues the muscles. As a result, they cannot perform their specific functions that allow normal, healthy movement of the shoulder.

You cannot control the congenital (anatomical) and acquired (arthritic) conditions that lead to impingement and injury but you can train and strengthen your muscles to reduce the fatigue and muscle imbalance that can predispose to injury. By strengthening your external rotators and scapular stabilizers, and by working on improving your stroke mechanics, you can reduce the intrinsic strain of this sport on your shoulders. In the weight room avoid military press and bench press. There are many other shoulder exercises that, if done with relatively light weights and increasing repetition, will condition the rotator cuff muscles to endure the rigours of dragon boat training and racing.

In summary, dragon boating is a sport with a great potential for injury, especially from repetitive strain and poor technique. A good pre-season conditioning program, a great deal of attention paid to good stroke mechanics, listening to your body, and ignoring the "no pain no gain" anthem, will best prepare you to steer around the rough waters of injury that dragon boaters might experience, and allow you to safely enjoy this wonderful sport.

Notes

1. Preparticipation Physical Evalution Working Group, *Preparticipation Physical Evaluation Monograph,* 3rd ed. (Minneapolis: McGraw-Hill Healthcare Information, 2004).
2. S. Hulkower, et al., "Do Preparticipation Clinical Exams Reduce Morbidity and Mortality for Athletes?" *Journal of Family Practice* 54 (2005), 28–32.
3. B.J. Maron, et al., "Sudden Death in Young Competitive Athletes: Clinical, Demographic and Pathological Profiles," *JAMA: The Journal of the American Medical Association*, Vol. 276 (1996), 199–204.
4. Modified version taken from "PAR-Q (Physical Activity-Readiness Questionnaire) Validation Report," British Columbia Department of Health, June 1975.
5. C.A. Richie and W.W. Briner, Jr., "Corticosteroid Injection for Treatment of de Quervain's Tenosynovitis: A Potential Quantitative Literature Evaluation," *Journal of American Board Family Practice*, Vol. 16, No. 2 (2003), 102–106.

Sources

Hulkower, S., et al. "Do Preparticipation Clinical Exams Reduce Morbidity and Mortality for Athletes?" *The Journal of Family Practice*, Vol. 54 (2005), 28–32.

Maron, B.J., et al. "Sudden Death in Young Competitive Athletes: Clinical, Demographic and Pathological Profiles." *JAMA: The Journal of the American Medical Association*, Vol. 276 (1996), 199–204.

PAR-Q (Physical Activity-Readiness Questionnaire) Validation Report, British Columbia Department of Health, June 1975.

Preparticipation Physical Evaluation Working Group. *Preparticipation Physical Evaluation Monograph,* 3rd ed. Minneapolis: McGraw-Hill Healthcare Information, 2004.

Richie, C.A., and W.W. Briner Jr. "Corticosteroid Injection for Treatment of de Quervain's Tenosynovitis: A Potential Quantitative Literature Evaluation." *Journal of American Board Family Practice*, Vol. 16, No. 2 (2003), 102–106.

10

龙 Nutrition 船

Pam Lumb Collett

Muscles require fuel to function and utilize energy from different chemical sources within the body. What is eaten, the frequency of meals, and the amount of food depend on factors like the intensity and volume of the activity. How quickly and efficiently these energy sources are mobilized can be changed through training and nutrition.

Nutrition is a complex and dynamic topic. Trends come and go and new information is unveiled daily, making it is impossible to include the latest and most up-to-date information. The word *diet* no longer implies "weight management"; rather it suggests a healthy eating lifestyle. This chapter will provide an overview of general principles and guidelines on nutrition to help you establish healthy eating habits and make better and more informed choices.

Individualized nutritional programs and topics like weight loss/gain, special dietary requirements, and eating disorders will not be discussed since these can best be addressed by sport and medical professionals.

ENERGY SYSTEMS

≠ ≭

Understanding how the body expends energy and how food provides fuel will help you select the appropriate foods before, during, and after practices, races, and regattas. Some foods provide and replenish energy stores more efficiently and effectively than others. Diet can also improve the rate of energy production and prepare muscles to efficiently deal with the waste products that accumulate during intense training.

Energy is expended all the time, even when you are sleeping. During exercise, there are three energy systems that the body uses in various combinations to produce energy, depending on such factors as the intensity and duration of the activity.

ANAEROBIC ALACTIC SYSTEM

≠ ≭

The anaerobic alactic system provides the primary energy for short, intense, and explosive power lasting up to 10 seconds, like that required at the start of a race. This startup system does not require oxygen nor does it produce lactic acid. The chemical breakdown of fuel into adenosine triphosphate (ATP), the source of about 95 percent of the body's energy requirements, results in a spark of energy that triggers muscle contraction. Diet and training can improve the ability of muscles to store energy.

ANAEROBIC LACTIC SYSTEM

≠ ⸯ

The anaerobic lactic system provides energy in the absence of oxygen for intense activities lasting more than 10 seconds. Glycogen stores are used to quickly produce more ATP and are depleted within 30 to 90 minutes depending on the intensity of the effort. This process also produces lactic acid, a by-product, that results in fatigue and a decrease in performance. Time is needed to recycle the lactic acid into an energy source so an "easy, light or flush paddle," rather than cessation of activity, is typically incorporated into training sessions. For race day, increasing blood glucose levels and stockpiling muscle glycogen can be improved through diet.

AEROBIC SYSTEM

≠ ⸯ

The aerobic (or respiration) system provides the energy to exercise continuously for extended periods of time. Oxygen is needed to convert carbohydrates, fats, and "recycled" lactic acid into ATP. The efficiency of this system is often referenced as cardiovascular fitness.

NUTRITION AND THE ATHLETE

≠ ⸯ

The nutritional needs of an athlete are not significantly different from the requirements of a healthy individual. The athlete consumes a higher percentage of carbohydrates (referred to as the "GO" food) and slightly elevated amounts of protein (referred to as the "GROW" food). Age, gender, activity level, body type, metabolic rate, and other factors determine the number of servings from the four food groups, as listed in *Canada's Food Guide*. As the ability to provide fuel more efficiently during training improves, appetite and the frequency of snacking will likely increase. The three main food sources that can be converted into ATP are protein, fat, and carbohydrates.

Protein

Protein, needed for growth and repair of body tissues, is important for both training and recovery from exercise. It is only used for energy in extreme situations when the body's carbohydrate and fat stores have been depleted.

Varying amounts are found in foods with complete proteins (those containing eight essential amino acids) derived mostly from animal products, such as, meat, fish, and eggs, and incomplete protein (lacking one or more essential amino acids) coming from sources like vegetables, fruit, and nuts.

Fat

Fat is the primary energy source during aerobic activities. However, because it takes longer than carbohydrates to break down into ATP, fat is not an efficient food source for paddlers. Fats are classified into "good fats," known as essential fatty acids, and "bad fats," like saturated and trans fat. "Bad fats" should be limited in the diet of an athlete.

Carbohydrates

Carbohydrates are an important energy source for an active person. They provide a rich source of vitamins, minerals, and fibre. *Canada's Food Guide* recommends a daily serving of at least one orange vegetable, such as sweet potatoes, carrots, or squash, and one dark-green vegetable, such as broccoli, chard, *gai lan* (Chinese broccoli), romaine lettuce, or spinach.

A 1:1 ratio of carbohydrate to body weight is a simple formula to calculate the daily amount of carbohydrates recommended for paddlers. For example, 50 grams of carbohydrate is recommended for a paddler weighing 50 kilograms.

Carbohydrates are classified as simple or complex, according to the speed at which they are converted to glucose. Simple carbohydrates taste sweet; complex carbohydrates are starchy, like potatoes.

Simple Carbohydrates

Simple carbohydrates are absorbed and metabolized relatively quickly. This process provides the body with a fast but short burst of energy, often followed by an energy low. Since insulin transfers nutrients from the bloodstream at the cellular level, replenishing insulin levels with simple sugars drives more nutrients into the bloodstream and replenishes glycogen stores rapidly. Eating simple carbohydrates within 30 minutes (or sooner!) after activity helps with muscle recovery and replaces glycogen stores quickly.

Simple carbohydrates occur naturally in fruits and, to a lesser extent, in vegetables. Natural simple carbohydrates include sugars found in fruit (fructose) and in milk (galactose and lactose). Processed carbohydrates that are present in sugary soft drinks, sugary cereals, white bread, white sugar, ice cream, white rice, and most commercial bakery products, are often referred to as "bad carbs" because they are empty calories.

Labels on commercial baked goods, chocolate bars or soft drinks usually have ingredients ending in "ose" at the top of the list. The main ingredients in these processed foods, many of which also contain trans fat, are simple carbohydrates.

Complex Carbohydrates

Complex carbohydrates break down slowly, sustain the feeling of being full, and provide constant energy for prolonged periods of time. Complex carbohydrates are found naturally in starchy vegetables, fruits, whole grains, brown rice, nuts, soy products, and legumes. They contain dietary fibres that are categorized as high fibre or low fibre.

High-fibre complex carbohydrates are found in green plants, like vegetables, and contain cellulose that is not digestible by humans. As a result, these have the capacity to keep the stomach feeling full with zero calories. Products containing two grams of fibre per 100 grams are considered high-fibre foods. Extra fluids are needed to help with their digestion. Whole fruits (with skin and pulp) have natural fibre that allows the efficient absorption of sugars

Low-fibre complex carbohydrates can be found in natural foods, like bananas, tomatoes, squash, and potatoes. Processed food made with white floor, such as doughnuts, cookies, crackers, bread, rolls, and pasta, also are sources of low-fibre carbohydrates; however, these refined foods should be minimized in a healthy diet.

Some athletes load up on carbohydrates, a process called "carb loading," to increase glycogen stores. This practice may improve performance in high endurance sports that require 90 minutes or more of non-stop effort, like marathons; however, it may not be as effective for paddlers. Excess carbohydrates that are not used during exercise convert into fat.

Large helpings of simple carbohydrates can disturb sleep patterns because of the sugar high. Complex carbohydrates take time to digest and can also disrupt sleep.

GLYCEMIC INDEX
$$\neq \neq$$

The glycemic index (GI) ranks foods on a scale from 0 to 100 according to the extent to which they raise blood sugar levels. The index provides another way at classifying carbohydrates. Foods with a high GI (simple carbohydrates) release glucose into the bloodstream quickly, thereby causing blood sugar levels to rise rapidly. Conversely, foods with a low GI (complex carbohydrates) release glucose more steadily over several hours and help to keep blood sugar levels relatively calm.

Low GI foods are usually high-fibre foods that are lower in calories and rich in nutrients and antioxidants. Generally, the lower the GI rating is, the higher the quality of carbohydrate. The following chart gives examples of foods and their GI rankings.

Hydration

≠ ≭

During exercise, body temperature increases. Sweating is the natural cooling system of the body with the amount of fluid and minerals that are lost depending on each individual and the intensity and duration of the activity. Environmental conditions, like temperature and humidity, also affect the body's ability to dissipate heat. The basic rule of thumb is that if you are hot and sweating, that is good. If you are hot and not sweating, you are showing signs of overheating.

To prevent overheating, move to a cool and shady area and rehydrate with clear liquids frequently. If

Examples of Foods and GI Ranges

Classification	GI range	Examples
Low GI (complex carbs)	55 or less	most fruit and vegetables (except potatoes, watermelon), grainy breads, pasta, beans, chickpeas, lentils, basmati rice, milk
Medium GI	56 - 69	wheat bread, whole wheat products, brown rice, sweet potato, table sugar
High GI (simple carbs)	70 – 99	corn flakes, baked potato, some white rice (like jasmine), croissant, white bread, candy
	100	straight glucose

the weather is hot and dry or hot and humid, fluid replacement is essential.

Drink plenty of water or clear fluids up until approximately two hours before training. Dehydration can cause muscle cramps and a decrease in performance levels. Once you feel thirsty, dehydration is highly probable.

When practices last longer than 60 minutes or when the weather is hot, a sports drink[1] may be useful to replace the water, carbohydrates, and electrolytes that have been lost. Be aware that many sports drinks are high in calories and sugars. As an alternative, mix one part fruit or vegetable juice with two parts water and add a pinch of salt (only if you are sweating heavily or if the weather is extremely hot and humid). Try squeezing a few drops of lemon juice into a water bottle to make a rehydrating drink that also supplies carbohydrates and vitamin C. Coffee, tea, and alcohol dehydrate so these should be avoided or taken in limited quantities.

EATING WELL BEFORE, DURING, AND AFTER A RACE OR PRACTICE
≠ ≭

The training diet is the food consumed every day, all year round. A healthy diet provides fuel for training, promotes muscles to store more carbohydrates, and helps improve the conversion of fuel to energy. In general, fats and empty calories should be minimized. Cooking follows the "4 Bs": bake; boil; broil; BBQ. Fats and oils added during food preparation are avoided as unnecessary calories. Visible fat on meat is always trimmed. On toast, butter or margarine is substituted by jam or honey. Yogurt, instead of mayonnaise, is used in salad dressings. Sorbet (no fat) or sherbet (maximum 2 percent fat) replaces ice cream.

As race day approaches, these and other healthy eating habits should already be well established. The athlete is well rested, well fuelled, and well hydrated. Priorities on competition day include proper hydration and sufficient energy for the entire race event.

Foods to avoid are:

- High fat, low nutrient foods;
- Protein-rich foods;
- Processed refined foods;
- Spicy foods;
- Fibre-rich foods;
- Gas-producing foods, e.g., beans, cabbage, carbonated drinks;
- Cream soups;
- Fried foods (meats, fish, poultry, potatoes);
- Butter and cream sauces and soups;

- Processed meats that have high salt content;
- Salads with creamy dressings (potato, coleslaw, tuna);
- Alcohol, coffee, tea.

DIGESTION TIMES

≠ ≴

Digestion takes two to three hours and, of course, depends on the content and size of meals and snacks. Sufficient time for digestion is needed before a race or practice.

- Large Meal — three to four hours;
- Smaller Meal — two to three hours;
- Snacks, e.g., blender meal or fruit — one to two hours.

Eating five or six smaller meals throughout the day is preferable to eating three large meals. It is also better to eat the largest meal earlier in the day and smaller portions for the remainder of the day. Consuming low GI foods three hours before training and racing helps to regulate blood-sugar levels.

MEALS AND SNACKS BEFORE RACES AND PRACTICES

≠ ≴

New foods and menus should not be introduced close to race day. There is comfort in familiarity and pre-competition nerves tend to upset a sensitive stomach. Carbohydrates provide the primary source of energy for activity, and protein is needed for muscle growth and repair. Plan the menu accordingly. Limit fat and protein portions as they take longer to digest. Four hours before the activity, drink at least one mouthful of fluid for every kilogram of body weight. Coffee or tea is not included in the fluid count.

Since practice sessions, start times on race day, and times between races vary, breakfast, lunch, dinner, and snack suggestions are provided. In general, avoid any deep-fried and pan-fried foods.

Breakfast Suggestions

- Fruit with low acidity, e.g., peaches, pears, apricots, apples;
- Fruit juice;

- Yogurt — low-fat, plain or with fruit;
- Fruit smoothie — home-made with fruit juice, low-fat yogurt, and fresh fruit;
- French toast or pancakes and maple syrup or honey — with no added butter or margarine;
- Eggs — boiled or poached;
- Ham or steak — lean; small portions;
- Potatoes — no added butter or margarine;
- Rice — steamed or boiled;
- Pasta, noodles — cooked al dente with tomato or vegetable sauce;
- Toast or bagel — with jam, jelly, or honey; no butter or margarine;
- Chocolate milk — 1 percent;
- Beverages — at least one glass.

Lunch and Dinner Suggestions

- Fruit and vegetables — fresh, juice, canned;
- Soups — broth, not cream;
- Fish, poultry — lean, skin removed from poultry, visible fat trimmed, small portions;
- Cold cuts — lean; fresh preferred to processed;
- Vegetables — steamed, boiled, baked, roasted;
- Potatoes — not fried, no added butter or margarine;
- Rice — steamed or boiled;

- Pasta — cooked al dente with tomato or vegetable sauce;
- Bread — rolls, crackers, whole-grain;
- Salads — fresh vegetables or fruit with low-fat cottage cheese, limited dressing.

One Hour (or Less) Before Race or Before Practice

- Fruit;
- Juice, e.g., orange, tomato, or V-8;
- Chocolate milk — 1 percent;
- Water.

Two to Three Hours Before Race or Practice

- Fruit;
- Fruit or vegetable juices;
- Bread, bagels;
- Low-fat yogurt;
- Water.

Three to Four Hours Before Race or Practice

- Fruit;
- Fruit or vegetable juices;
- Bread, bagels;
- Pasta with tomato sauce;
- Baked potatoes;
- Cereal with low-fat milk;
- Low-fat yogurt;
- Toast or bread with limited peanut butter, lean meat, or low-fat cheese;
- Water.

Between Races, After the Race, After Practice, or at the End of the Day

Fluid replacement is the priority. Drink plenty of water, diluted fruit juices or sports drinks to refuel the body with carbohydrate-rich foods for recovery. Eating carbohydrates within 15 minutes after a race or practice stimulates insulin production that, in turn, stimulates the production of glycogen. The body is at its highest rate of absorbency and delivery of nutrients in this time period. Snacks with small quantities of carbohydrates are especially important if there is a delay in the start of the event or there is a long wait between races. Fruit (especially bananas), low-fat granola bars, low-fat yogurt, Fig Newtons, almonds, diluted fruit juice, and pretzels are good choices to snack on throughout the day. A balance of protein for muscle repair and fats for absorption of nutrients should be included in the post-event menu.

CONCLUSION

Sports nutrition is a complex subject that lends itself to conflicting information and research and to discussion beyond the scope of this chapter. See your doctor or other health care professional for nutrition advice that is individualized for your specific needs. What is most important to remember is eating a balanced diet and drinking enough water. These are the key factors in making your body more energy efficient. Maintaining good dietary habits will contribute to your ability to perform your personal best, including your rate of recovery following activity.

Drink plenty of fluids, eat healthy, paddle fit!

NOTES

1. Sports drinks and other related products, like e-gels, are designed to maintain hydration and electrolyte and carbohydrate balance. Supplements are a major topic of debate beyond the scope of this chapter.

SOURCES

Bean, Anita. *Complete Guide to Sports Nutrition*, 5th ed. London: A & C Black, 2006.

BodySense: A Positive Body Image Initiative for Athletes. Accessed at *www.bodysense.ca/about_us/index_e.html.*

Caulfield, Carol Anne. *Sport Nutrition for the Athletes of Canada: Workbook for Athletes.* Gloucester, ON: Sport Medicine Council of Canada, 1993.

Coaching Association of Canada. *Sports nutrition.* Accessed at *www.coach.ca/eng/nutrition/index.cfm.*

Coaching Association of Canada. *National Coaching Certification Program: Multi-Sport Modules.* Gloucester, ON: Coaching Association of Canada, 2007.

Health Canada. *Canada's Food Guide.* Ottawa, ON: Health Canada, 2007. Accessed at *www.hc-sc.gc.ca/fn-an/food-guide-ailment/index-eng.php.*

Sensible Nutrition Connection. Accessed at *www.sensiblenutrition.com/index.html.*

11

The International Standard Dragon Boat: Canadian Content

龙　　　船

Mike Kerkmann

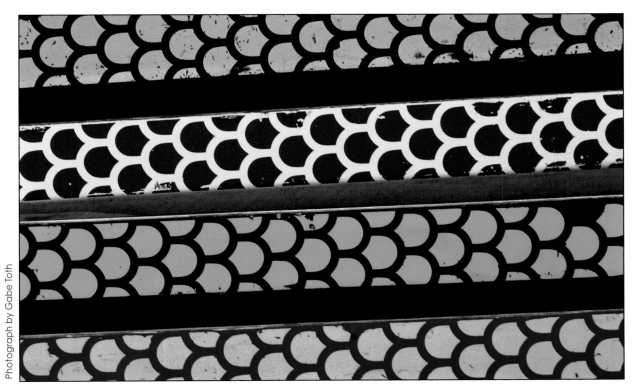

Photograph by Gabe Toth

The brightly coloured patterns on these boats represent the scales of the dragon.

If you ask your average Canadian "what is our national sport?" the vast, vocal majority will immediately and confidently blurt out "hockey." I recall this question being directed at three high-IQ Americans appearing on the popular game show *Jeopardy*, and yes, all the contestants buzzed with the same thought … ice hockey. The host of the show, Canada's own Alex Trebek, seemed tickled that the "trick" question had fooled his American friends. "That distinction," he mused, "belongs to field lacrosse!" Now, if you're congratulating yourself, thinking you were aware of this little bit of trivia, guess what, you're wrong … and you're right too. Up until 1994, lacrosse was,

indeed, Canada's national sport, but the National Sports of Canada Act, introduced in May of that year, confirmed that lacrosse was Canada's official *summer* sport and that hockey was added as Canada's official *winter* sport. The reason I have introduced the chapter with this factoid is to point out that one, Her Majesty, the Senate, and House of Commons can dicker with Canada's national sport designations, and two, I think dragon boat racing should be considered as Canada's new national *water sport*.

Punch "dragon boat" into any popular on-line search engine. After Wikipedia gets its two cents in, the next 50 (I stopped counting) hits are Canadian festivals and clubs. If you are reading this book, I likely don't need to reaffirm Canada's national team and club crew prominence at the international level. Dragon boat racing is, indeed, Canada's fastest-growing national summer pastime.

What many readers may not realize is that Canadians, particularly those involved in our dynamic dragon boat commercial sector, have played a defining role in developing the international standard dragon boat, and also in the evolution of the standard PS202a paddle. I begin with my own story.

In June 1988, I stepped onto a dock at Toronto's Ontario Place and was handed a short wooden paddle by a smiling Asian woman who gestured toward a long teakwood vessel called a dragon boat. The team that adopted me was the Hong Kong Lions Club and I was a fill-in, invited by my then girlfriend and presented as someone who was fit but not a paddler. Turns out this was a pretty good team of marathon canoers who were intent on beating those dastardly sprint paddlers to claim the prize of a trip for 20 to race in Hong Kong. Alas, it was not to be. But, like many of you, I fell hard and fast for the sport and spent the next few years racing with the likes of the Chinese Cultural Centre and Sunnybrook Hospital Teams. One common and chronic issue during the early 1990s was the difficulty we had with securing regular access to one of the 12 dragon boats owned

by the organization that produced Toronto's annual dragon boat festival, the Toronto Chinese Business Association (TCBA). It was at this time that dragon boats and my life became conjoined.

In the years preceding the introduction of dragon boats to Canada, my entrepreneurial father had invested in constructing a furniture factory in Honduras, Central America. Intermixed with employment and university commitments, I would spend several weeks each winter working with my father retooling the factory and developing new products. In the fall of 1992, some of my crewmates suggested that it would be a fine idea to build the team its own dragon boat while I was in Honduras that coming winter. Interestingly, I never considered, at the time, that fibreglass, or even a plywood hull, made any sense. The goal was to construct a replica of the 910-kilogram teak boat that we had been training and racing in for the past four years. Seemed simple enough. With trusty tape measure in hand, I gained access to the TCBA boats being stored in a Toronto Portland warehouse and sketched out the boat. Some may have wondered how I planned to build a replica teak boat when teak is indigenous only to South Asia. Well, as fate would have it, Honduras was the only Western country to have introduced plantation teak to its managed forests many decades ago. Fast forward to the spring of 1993, which saw

Photograph by Jan Oakley

Traditional dragon boats can carry as many as 80 people although there still exists, in China, a boat that can hold up to 300 people. This one, pictured on the east coast of Canada, is a modern boat with the standard capacity for 20 paddlers, one drummer, and one steersperson.

the proud launch of two plantation-teak, replica dragon boats into the Humber River basin near Toronto's waterfront. While the original intent of constructing these two boats was not commercially based, one promptly sold for $10,000 and the other quickly booked itself to capacity with crews training for the 1993 version of the Toronto International Dragon Boat Festival.

In the spring of 1994, three additional Honduran-built teak boats were introduced into the fleet. Team rentals and festival leasing opportunities in Toronto, Guelph, Hamilton, and London emerged, and Great White North Dragon Boat Racing was born. Over the course of the next five years, the hull design and construction materials of the Great White North (GWN) boat moved away from the traditional Hong

Kong–style teak boat. The second generation of GWN boats was constructed in 1997 with marine plywood and epoxy resins. These were 10 percent larger than past designs and all are still in service today. On the West Coast, Vincent Lo at Six-Sixteen had introduced his even larger fibreglass dragon boat. The general theme of the time was that the traditional teak boat suited (some would say favoured) the typical Asian dragon boat crew, but North American and European paddlers needed a larger boat to accommodate larger athletes, not to mention the occasional borderline-obese festival participant! Meanwhile, the TCBA direction was to blend traditional design with modern materials. A teak boat was presented to Voyageur Canoe Company in Millbrook, Ontario, with instructions to make a mould and to construct six fibreglass versions of the Hong Kong–style boat for use in future Toronto International Dragon Boat Race Festival events.

While Canada rushed into developing the dragon boat corporate/community festival model coast to coast, a different and more regularized approach took hold in Europe. The first three Hong Kong–style teak dragon boats arrived in London in 1980 as window dressing for the Hong Kong in London Chinese Festival. Current IDBF executive president Mike Haslam and friends introduced dragon boating to the canoe-kayak racing community in those early years by co-organizing races at various venues in the United Kingdom. At the time the notion was that dragon boating could, and should, naturally become a discipline of canoeing by way of association with the British Canoe Union (BCU) and, by affiliation, the International Canoe Federation (ICF). When confronted with general disinterest by BCU and ICF types, Mike and company struck out on their own. In 1986, Chris Hare Marine took a mould of the Hong Kong–style teak boat so that less-expensive, lighter-weight fibreglass boats could be produced and shipped to various European countries interested in expanding the sport.

In 1991, the International Dragon Boat Federation (IDBF) was formed, followed by continental federations in Asia and Europe. Together these sport organizations developed founding principles, one of which was to adopt the traditional hull design that had been used at the Hong Kong International Races since the mid-1970s for international sport racing.

At the same time, with the inception of the British Dragon Boat Association and European Dragon Boat Federation, a commission was struck to refine the specification by way of recording the detailed measurements of a Hong Kong–style hull to create a derivative, computer-based model. Under the watchful eye of the German Dragon Boat Association, Boots und Kunststoffbau (BuK) of Germany constructed

Photograph by Jan Oakley

The IDBF has two sanctioned models of International Racing Dragon Boats. The first, like the one used by 22Dragons in Montreal, Quebec, is designed for a crew of 22 people. The second model is designed for crews of 12 or less.

the first European Standard Dragon Boat plug, mould, and hull in 1993, and, in 1994, the IDBF adopted the design. The International Standard Dragon Boat was born!

In the summer of 1999, Canadian dragon boat racing was in full swing, though crews were still racing in wooden boats or heavy, ill-fitting, Hong Kong–fibreglass copies. GWN was producing over a dozen festivals in Canada. Marquee spring festivals in Ottawa, Toronto, and Vancouver were bursting at the seams. The Great White North Challenge had grown to over 100 teams and was the sport's key, season-ending competition. A few years earlier, in 1996, Canada had become the first nation, outside of Asia, to win the prestigious World Championship Premier Open event in Hong Kong. The victory was significant in that it created a new optic for Canada and the rest of the world. The Western world could beat the previously dominant Chinese at their own game! Canada's national team coaches returned home confident they could repeat the feat at the 1997 IDBF World Dragon Boat Racing Championships. Funding flowed through the TCBA rank and file and the 1997 National Crew enjoyed similar success, though they finished a controversial second to the U.S. National Team.

In 1999, I decided it was time to see, for myself, what all this international racing fuss was about. What was largely a last minute decision, I boarded a plane to London and hopped on a train headed for Nottingham for the 3rd IDBF World Dragon Boat Racing Championships. I arrived on day two of competition, settled into a corner of the regatta control centre, and started taking notes. Then came a series of fateful encounters. I began snooping around the athletes' village where I had a brief encounter with Canada's Premier Open Crew's head coach, Jim Farintosh. I had never met Jim before that day but I was aware of his involvement with the TCBA program back in Toronto. Jim expressed great concern with the boats that were being provided by the championship organizers. While the organizing committee had undoubtedly done its best to assemble a credible racing fleet for the competition, it was, in reality, a jumble of boats of different years, makes, and models, including split boats[1] (yuk!). In the Team Canada tent, there was plenty of anxiety to go around when it appeared certain that the open crew would be assigned the appropriately nicknamed yellow "banana boat" for the final race of the afternoon. This particular boat, when observed broadside, was noticeably more rocky than the other boats in the fleet. And this was a significant handicap in the eyes of Jim and the rest of the coaching staff. The boat had already developed a reputation as a loser. The other curious design element of the Euro-style boat was that the interior seat configuration included 13 benches. I found this to be strange. These 13 benches, or 26 paddler seats, created a mildly entertaining, musical-chair dynamic as crews heading to the start line shifted paddlers up and down the boat from seat to seat to try and achieve the best possible fore-aft balance. Coaches were jogging along the racecourse shouting at their crews to move athletes back a seat or up a seat. Very strange indeed. And to make matters worse, every second seat featured a fully enclosed, cross-sectional bulkhead, leaving little room for half of the athletes to extend and brace their feet forward. That night, I tossed and turned but I had a plan.

On day two, I crossed around to the far side of the regatta course to introduce myself to some of these 13-bench dragon boat builders. There were

Photograph by Jens Ronneberger

During a race event, like the 2006 Club Crew World Championships in Toronto, Ontario, three sets of boats are typically used. One set will be ready at the docks for loading, one will be racing down the course, and the third set will be approaching or jockeying into positions at the start line.

three manufacturers on site that week, and I have to say honestly that North America's first experience with the international standard boat could have easily been with any one of the three. And I have to say openly that it was nothing more than intuition, my gut, that drew me back to the BuK boat display a third and fourth time. Now, the BuK Stankewitz brothers, Andreas and Roland, did not initially welcome me with open arms. My initial suggestion to become an "exclusive" North American distributor for their product was rebuffed. I told them that I was interested in the boat but not the fully built version. I was interested in just the shells of the boats and wanted to import these so I could build the interior the way I wanted … with 10 benches. I'm pretty sure, by the look I received, that they were thinking "who is this

Canadian who wants to bastardize our boat?!" The other rough edge cutting painfully into my plan was that the United States Dragon Boat Federation had gotten to BuK first, had enquired about distribution, and had committed to a container of completed boats to Philadelphia in the spring of 2000.

Now, I'm not sure why the BuK brothers had a change of heart, but at the celebration party that Sunday night, they brought a rather large bottle of wine over to my table, sat down, and, by the time our glasses were empty, we had a distribution deal in place. The one condition was that a single container of Euro-style, 13-bench boats, destined for Philadelphia, would proceed as planned … and that was just fine by me.

Upon my return to Canada, the focus was on the layout of the interior of the boat. At the time, I had no particular interest in adhering to the IDBF specification. In 1999, formal sport racing was a non-issue in Canada. The key to the success of the product in North America was, in my view, festival paddler comfort. This meant a spacious seat area to stretch one's legs and extend one's arms. My brief encounter with this Farintosh fellow in Nottingham told me a couple of things. One, he knew what he was talking about when it came to making a dragon boat go fast. Two, if approached to help me design an alternative to the notorious Euro, 13-bench boat for North America, he would be sufficiently motivated, given his experiences in Nottingham.

It was the fall of 1999 and in the tradition of big ideas on café napkins, the redesign of interior bulkheads and balanced seat spacing for the first generation BuK North American dragon boat took place in Jim's living room in the Toronto Beaches neighbourhood.

In the early spring of 2000, the first container of BuK shells arrived in Toronto and was delivered to my good friend and marine craftsman, Bill Burek. Bill, who had been building GWN's second generation wooden dragon boats for the past three years, used his considerable skill to retrofit the BuK shells with solid and marine-ply mahogany inlays and seats. On a crisp day in May of that year, the world's first BuK 10-bench boat was lowered into Toronto's shipping channel for its first test run that featured a group of national crew athletes assembled by Jim. The boat did precisely what it was designed to do. It went fast, it was comfortable and well balanced … and damn good looking too!

By the fall of 2000, the impact of my Nottingham trip, BuK distribution agreement, and napkin-sketching sessions on the development of the International Standard Dragon Boat had yet to flush out internationally, but one thing was certain. The boat quickly set and became the standard in North America. In less than one year, 30 BuK boats had

Photograph by Heather Maclaren

Dragon boats, like these ones awaiting the finals of the False Creek Women's Regatta in Vancouver, British Columbia, are 12 metres in length.

been retrofitted and sold across Canada and the U.S. GWN's own fleet featured 12 brand-new BuK NorAm dragon boats.

The winter of 2001 saw a series of events begin to shape the coming of the 4th IDBF Dragon Boat World Championships awarded to New York City … or wait, was that Philadelphia? Yes it was, but only after the IDBF visited the originally awarded venue at Flushing Lake in New York City and rejected it, primarily because of lack of water depth sufficient to host a world championship regatta. Bob Morro, then

secretary of the United States Dragon Boat Federation, suggested the nearby Schuylkill River Regatta Course in Philadelphia. After some deliberation, an agreement was reached that the event would be moved to this new venue. There was a problem; no International Standard Racing Dragon Boat (ISRDB) fleet existed in the eastern United States and the event was less than 10 months away. In the spring of 2001, I received a call from the chair of the 4th IDBF World Championship Organizing Committee and a deal was struck for GWN to provide the entire racing fleet for the championships. It was at this event that I had a most interesting conversation with Mike Haslam regarding the BuK NorAm dragon boat. In all honesty, I assumed Mike would be pleased with this new, sensible interior layout for the ISRDB. In fact, I was certain that many of the positive comments I received from the various European teams, including the captain of the British team, had filtered back to him. So, I was surprised to get a bit of a tongue-lashing from him. It seems that the IDBF was not interested in revising the specification for the boat and Mike actually expressed his annoyance that I would just go forward and revise the seat spacing in "their" boat, all on my own, without any consultation with the IDBF whatsoever.

Meanwhile, the approval rating for the boat did not go unnoticed by the Stankewitz brothers who had made the trip to Philadelphia. I am sure it was, at that point, when Andreas began to conceive the design for the next generation of the BuK International Standard boat.

Over the next three years, NorAm BuKs sold at a remarkable rate and continued to impress European crews who travelled to Canada to compete in our festivals. Over 140 first-generation NorAm BuKs were sold before the company introduced its second-generation, 10-bench design to the world. In actual fact, the boat was introduced and was raced initially in Canada and the United States in the spring of 2005 and wouldn't be unveiled in Europe until September at the European championships in Prague. It didn't take long for the remaining manufacturers in Europe and Asia, and for the IDBF, to recognize, that the BuK design, which incorporated the Canadian-version interior layout, represented the future of international dragon boat racing. The IDBF, eventually and quietly, retired the 13-bench boat and released the revised "Canada content … shhhh!" specification. So, ladies and gentlemen, think about that the next time you check your paddle on an international flight over to goodness-knows-where. Canadian forethought and ingenuity have made your domestic and global dragon boat racing experience infinitely more comfortable, faster, and, ultimately, more rewarding.

NOTES

1. **Editor's Note:** A dragon boat with a hull that is designed to be dismantled into two halves of approximately equal length for transport.

龙 12

Dragon Boat Paddles 船

Gerry Kavanagh

Fifteen years ago only a small handful of manufacturers were producing paddles specific to dragon boat racing, and almost all of them were made of wood. The paddles varied greatly in wood selection, quality, and consistency. Fast-forward to 2008, and the tremendous worldwide growth in popularity with recreational and serious sport paddlers has seen an equally tremendous growth in the number of manufacturers that now offer dragon boat paddles in a variety of prices and construction materials. This has created a lot of competition among manufacturers and generated many questions from paddlers trying to distinguish the differences and choose a paddle.

IDBF Specification 202a Paddles

$$\neq \; \not\equiv$$

The intent of the International Dragon Boat Federation is that dragon boat races should be won by the training and efforts of the crew and not because of the technical superiority of the equipment that is used. The purpose of creating a specification for paddles is to standardize the design of the equipment in order to provide fair competition for crews at all levels within the sport. The IDBF has introduced an approval system for dragon boat paddles made to the IDBF Racing Paddle specification. The system is known as the "IDBF Members' Racing Paddle Scheme,"[1] designed for purchasers of dragon boat paddles to identify the ones made to IDBF specification and thus approved for use in competitions held under IDBF regulations.

The Racing Paddle Scheme was first introduced by the European Dragon Boat Federation in 1994 to encourage manufacturers to build dragon boat paddles to a standard specification. The IDBF adopted the scheme in 1997 for worldwide use by its members and now classifies all paddles made to specification as "International Standard Racing Paddles." The Specification 202a paddle is the latest version of the Standard Racing Paddle and is the current standard for international competition. All Specification 202a approved paddles are identified by the IDBF-issued licence number appearing on the blade or shaft. See the list of IDBF licensed racing paddle manufacturers.

An example of a drawing for the IDBF Specification 202a paddle is shown in Figure 1. The specification is strict on the size and dimensions of the blade and overall length of the paddle. For example, the shoulder is a specific radius; the tips and edges have a minimum and maximum thickness; the blade cross section must be convex; and the paddle must be symmetrical so that it can be used identically forward and backward.

IDBF Licensed Racing Paddle Manufacturers - Spec 202a
As of January 2008

Manufacturer	Country of Origin	IDBF Licence Number	Email
Apex Composites	Canada	3021/22/23	info@apexpaddles.com
Braca Sport Ltd.	Lithuania	3061	braca-hu@braca-sport.com
Burnwater	USA	3011	arinchang@burnwater.com
Chinook Paddles	Canada	3131	info@chinookpaddles.com
ES Dragon Paddles	Germany	3101	Brigitte.Schmidt@beiersdorf.com
Grey Owl	Canada	3081/82/83	info@greyowlpaddles.com
G´Power	Poland	3121	info@gpower.pl
Land & Ocean Composites	China	3111	lando@land-ocean.net
Ocky Oars	Australia	3071	edmcilwain@bigpond.com
RAAB Paddles	Czech Republic	3141	raab@cmail.cz
Simon River Sports	Canada	3091/92/93	lou@simonriversports.com
Swift International	China	3151	timyang@swiftinternational.biz
Talon Technology	Australia	3201	geoff@talon.com.au
Trivium	Lithuania	3051	info@triviumpaddles.com
Typhoon 8	Hong Kong	3041/3042	lister@typhoon8.com
ZRE Racing	USA	3031	zaveralb@mkl.com

Wood paddles are provided at a race regatta organized by Dragon Boat East.

One even more important area of freedom is in construction materials.

Figure 1: IDBF Spec 202a Paddle

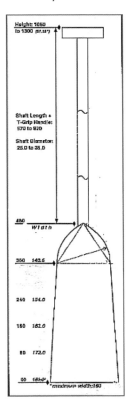

Although the dimensions are strictly controlled, there are a few areas of freedom including the handle style and the shape of the shaft (oval or round).

CONSTRUCTION MATERIALS
≠ ≠

Wood

Wood paddles are generally constructed by laminating different types of hardwoods with resin, shaped with machines (and/or by hand), and then treated with a layer of fibreglass on the blade. Some of the less expensive wood paddles are only treated with varnish.

The cost, weight, and performance of wood paddles can vary greatly based on the selection of wood and number of laminations. There are also some hybrid wood paddles being built that offer a wood blade and handle, but a carbon fibre or fibreglass shaft. Weights of wood and wood hybrid paddles can range from around 600 grams to almost 1 kilogram. Purchase price can also vary from $35 to $120.

There are still a number of manufacturers building wood dragon boat paddles. Wood paddles have the advantage of being flexible and inexpensive. This makes them a natural choice for clubs and fleet owners, as the initial cost is manageable, and for new paddlers who are looking for their own equipment, but are not ready to spend a lot of money on their new hobby. On the downside, they can wear out quickly if used a lot, and become waterlogged and split between their laminations. For clubs, this can mean replacement every one to two years. If a wood paddle is taken care of properly, it can offer years of service. Many paddlers believe that wood gives them the best "feel" of the water and do not believe in using anything else!

Plastic

There have been a few plastic paddles and plastic hybrids introduced recently, but most are sold as club or training paddles as they do not meet Specification 202a. Typically, these are offered as injection moulded blades with aluminum shafts. These paddles are usually

Carbon fibre is a material made with thin fibres of carbon atoms. The crystal alignment of the atoms makes the material strong for its size and featherweight.

heavy and the aluminum shafts tend to bend and stay bent. Although they are fairly inexpensive, these are ineligible for use in most dragon boat races.

Composite/Carbon Fibre

One of the most exciting developments in dragon boat paddles is the introduction of carbon fibre. There are at least 15 manufacturers now producing Specification 202a carbon fibre composite paddles, some in two or more models.

The interesting part about these paddles is that although they all meet the same specification and are made of basically the same material, each has a unique feel. Weights for carbon fibre paddles start at 300 grams and go right up to almost 600 grams.

This carbon fibre paddle features a lightweight, one-piece construction with 100 percent carbon.

Composite materials used in dragon boat paddles are typically carbon fibre, fibreglass, and Kevlar. The resins used are mostly epoxy, and most paddles have some sort of foam core.

The use of composites in paddles allows manufacturers to tailor the performance characteristics. For instance, the use of more fibres longitudinally versus width-wise can create a stiffer paddle. By putting various layers of carbon fibre in certain areas and using different fibre orientations, the way in which the paddle absorbs and releases the load can be dramatically different. These decisions will also have a great effect on the weight and durability of the paddle.

One common misconception is that carbon fibre is indestructible. This is not really true. Although it is many times stronger than steel on a kilogram for kilogram basis, carbon fibre is stiff and thus brittle. Manufacturers must

This high-performance paddle is constructed with an extra stiff carbon shaft and a fibreglass-covered blade made from hardwood.

choose between strength, durability, and weight when designing their paddles. The lightest carbon fibre paddle will almost certainly be less durable than the heaviest. Composite paddles range in price from $100 to $250.

CHOOSING A PADDLE

≠ ≠

Choosing a paddle is a difficult and personal decision. *There is no single paddle that is perfectly suited to everyone.* Here are some important features or characteristics to consider when choosing:

Stiffness

How stiff is the paddle? Does it hurt your joints? Do you like a direct connection to the water, or do you like the paddle to absorb some of the shock? A stiffer paddle generally transfers more energy into the boat, but it is a trade-off between power and comfort.

Weight

Do you want a feather or a hammer? Do you like minimum weight for an easier recovery phase of the stroke, or do you prefer the inertia of a heavier paddle?

Entry

Does the paddle enter cleanly into the water or plunk? A thinner tip creates a cleaner entry. There are minimum and maximum thicknesses allowed for the tip of the blade. Some blades are at the minimum while others are thicker than necessary.

Feel

How does the paddle track? Does it feel like there is good connection? Does it wobble at any point of the stroke? Is the shaft size and shape comfortable? Do you prefer a T-grip or a palm grip?

Balance

Is the weight distribution of the paddle comfortable

Handle with a T-grip.

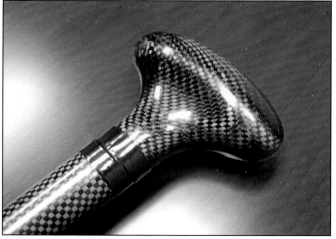

Handle with a palm grip.

Courtesy of Apex Composites

Courtesy of Apex Composites

for you? Is it weighted toward the tip, handle, or fairly even?

Budget

How much are you willing to spend? This can be one of the most important criteria as your budget will dictate what paddles are available in your price range.

Coaches are perhaps the most valuable resource when making the final decision. It is best to consult them because their coaching style will have an impact as to what paddle to choose, especially when considering the correct length.

NOTES

1. **Editor's Note:** Much of the original work in developing the specifications for the IDBF Racing Paddle Scheme was done by Canadians, including Mike Kerkmann and Adrian Lee.

SOURCES

International Dragon Boat Federation. *IDBF Licensed Racing Paddle Manufacturers — Spec 202a.* 2008. Accessed at *www.idbf.org/documents_licensed.php.*

International Dragon Boat Federation. *International Racing Paddle Scheme.* 2005. Accessed at *www.idbf.org/documents/Racing_Paddle_Scheme.pdf.*

13

Dragon Boat Racing:
A Guide to Safety
on the Water

龙　　船

Editor's Note: In 2007, a tragedy occurred when five dragon boat paddlers from the Singaporean Dragon Boat Crew lost their lives during a race competition in Phnom Penh, Cambodia. There were many unfortunate factors that, in combination, caused their boat to capsize. The safety of dragon boating cannot be overemphasized. To this end, an excerpt that has been adapted from *Annex A to the IDBF Water Safety Policy, International Dragon Boat Federation Members Handbook*, 5th ed., 2008, is included with permission from IDBF.

This guide is primarily for those organizing or competing in the sport of dragon boat racing. It covers their responsibilities when participating in a dragon boat event and should therefore be used as a general guide to "Safety on the Water" in a competitive situation. (In a non-competitive situation *and when training*, it is recommended that all participants and the activity organizer, also follow the general advice given in this guide.) For IDBF-sanctioned competitions, this guide forms part of the IDBF competition regulations and is to be read in conjunction with both the IDBF competition regulations and the rules of racing.

THE CONDITIONS
≠ ≯

Because of the size and design of the dragon boat, and the water conditions in which racing takes place, that is, placid water, dragon boating is inherently safe and a capsize especially in such conditions, unless the crew is at fault, is a rarity.

However, in any water sport, because of the environment itself, there is always an element of danger. Add to this the folly and impatience of human nature and the ingredients for an accident may eventually come together to the detriment of the sport as a whole. Dragon boat racing is no exception to the rule and it is the duty of all who practise the sport — competitors, race organizers, coaches, and officials alike — to be aware of the potential dangers inherent in the sport; to be safety conscious — not safety extreme — and to ensure that dragon boating is conducted in a responsible manner.

In adverse weather conditions and when there are strong winds, dragon boats can be swamped with water and have been known to capsize, especially when turning sideways on to the prevailing wind or wave pattern. In certain river conditions too, for example, when turning across a current of fast-moving water, if a crew is not experienced enough in such conditions a dragon boat can be subject to swamping or even capsize. The inexperience of the crew is normally a major factor if a boat capsizes in such conditions.

In all water conditions, good or bad, the key to safety is the application of good old COMMON SENSE by all those taking part in the activity. Playing around in a dragon boat and deliberately capsizing it, even in warm and sunny conditions, can be dangerous to both the crew and other water users alike. In certain circumstances it could be lethal; a dragon boat moving at speed through the water cannot easily be stopped and another crew

Photograph by Jens Ronneberger

The dock at the Great White North Dragon Boat Challenge, in Toronto, Ontario, provides an orderly area to pick up paddles and life jackets and to load the boats.

in the water from a capsized boat cannot easily be seen!

Crews that cause another boat to capsize when racing or ram another boat during a race will be disqualified from the event.

WHO IS RESPONSIBLE

≠ ≠

Dragon boat racing is a "team sport," and each boat carries a crew equivalent to two soccer teams. It is not unusual for nearly 100 competitors to be on the water, in one race. The safety of this number of competitors, at any one time, is the concern of many people but primarily the event organizer and the chief official. However, "Safety on the Water" is also the concern of every crew member.

THE RESPONSIBILITIES
≠ ≢

The broad areas of responsibility for safety are:

The Event Organizer

It is the event organizer's responsibility to ensure that adequate rescue boats, rescue personnel, and personal flotation aids (PFAs) are obtained for the event; that first-aid cover is provided off the water; that changing rooms, toilets and warm showers are provided and that all temporary structures comply with all regulations on such matters.

The event organizer shall ensure that crews are sent basic information on all safety matters appertaining to the competition.

The Chief Official

It is the chief official's responsibility to ensure that during the racing, all rescue boats are in place and briefed; that in all conditions competitors under 12 wear PFAs, and that in adverse water conditions PFAs are worn by known weak swimmers, Novice, and Junior competitors; and that in all conditions the IDBF safety procedures are complied with.

The Crew Manager

It is the crew manager's responsibility to ensure that all the crew members can swim to the required standard; that any weak swimmers are provided with PFAs; that the crew list is completed and lodged with the race secretary; that the crew is briefed on the racing rules and "Safety on the Water," and that, at all times, they are "fit to race." This means that it is the crew manager's responsibility to ensure that "socializing" does not adversely affect the performance of the crew on the water.

The Crew Members

It is the responsibility of the crew members to ensure

that when they are on the water they are adequately dressed for the weather conditions and comply with all instructions given to them. Dragon boating is a social sport too, so do not put the safety of the whole crew in jeopardy through alcohol, thoughtlessness or excessive horseplay.

The Helm (Boat Steerer)

The boat helm is normally the boat captain. It is the helm's responsibility to make the final check to ensure that the boat is water worthy and in racing condition and that all crew members are correctly briefed on boat handling and capsize drills. The Helm should also check that crew members are suitably dressed for the weather conditions and not wearing anything that may impede their ability to exit the boat or swim in the event of a capsize or boat swamping.

When on the water, the helm shall ensure that collisions with other craft are avoided. In the event of a boat swamping or capsizing, the helm shall ensure that the capsize drills are correctly carried out and that all competitors are accounted for and rescued.

SWIMMING — THE STANDARD REQUIRED

Ideally, all members in a dragon boat crew should be able to swim at least 50 metres, but as a minimum, they must be water competent in cold and moving water when dressed in light clothing, that is, racing dress (shorts and vest) plus waterproof top and trousers and light footwear (trainers, flip-flops, or similar footwear). (A person's swimming ability should be confirmed by testing, where possible, during training).

PERSONAL FLOATATION AIDS (PFAs) — WHEN TO WEAR THEM

In a formal competitive event and on a placid watercourse, in normal summer conditions, and providing that the individual can swim, the IDBF Rules of Racing do not require an experienced competitor to wear a personal floatation aid (PFA), such as a buoyancy aid. (This is in line with comparable water

Photograph by Jan Oakley

PFAs, or life jackets, are always available at regattas; however, many paddlers prefer to purchase their own.

sports.) Where local regulations at race site require water users to wear PFAs, all crews will wear them, irrespective of their experience in the sport. In such cases it is the event organizer's responsibility to notify crews whether or not the water operator provides PFAs and if NOT, it is the crew manager's responsibility to ensure that the crew has sufficient of their own to cater for any *water* conditions that they may encounter. However, even in perfect racing conditions, both the boat helm and drummer are advised to wear PFAs, and all competitors under the age of 12 years old must wear them. The event organizer should also provide PFAs for all other competitors who request them, or at the crew manager's request.

In an informal competitive event, such as a festival race, all competitors are advised to wear PFAs, which should be supplied by the event organizer concerned. In adverse racing (or training conditions) in temperate summer conditions, especially on open water or rivers, crew managers of experienced crews should advise all their competitors to wear PFAs and ensure that weak swimmers and those uncomfortable in such conditions do wear them. In any event, novice paddlers (those with less than one year of racing experience) and junior paddlers (those under 18 years) will wear PFAs in such conditions. When racing or training in cold water (temperate climate winter) conditions, all competitors are advised to wear PFAs.

SAFETY ON EMBARKATION
≠ ⩲

Boat Balance

Before leaving the embarking area, the boat captain (normally the helm) should ensure that the boat is well balanced. That is, each pair of racers are of similar weight or height and, generally, the heavier pairs are seated in the boat's middle section. ***The boat captain must know the number of people in the boat*** when the crew is embarked.

The Buddy System

The crew should be "numbered off" from the front of the boat and made aware that they are each responsible for the person they are paired with (across the boat) and that in the event of a capsize or the boat being swamped, their first responsibility is to ensure that their partner is safe and well. This is called the "buddy system" and it gives each person in the boat a specific responsibility for another. The "Stroke Pair" (first pair — No. 2 left and No. 3 right) in the boat are responsible for the drummer (1) and the "Rear Pair" (last pair) for the helm (22).

Steadying the Boat

A boat will feel "tippy" especially if the crew is out of balance or moving about in an uncoordinated manner. To steady the boat in such circumstances (and when sideways on to the wind or wave pattern) the crew should be instructed by the helm to slightly lean out over the side of the boat and place their paddle blades flat on the water, at arm's length. With all of the paddles on the water in this manner (10 either side) the boat is effectively stabilized. This is called a paddle brace and the helm's command should be "Brace the Boat."

Stopping the Boat

When manoeuvring, turning or racing, it may be necessary to stop the boat suddenly, say to avoid a collision with another vessel. It is important that the crew reacts quickly but safely. An unbalanced crew, overreacting, can capsize its own boat! The quickest way to stop a boat is for the crew to do a reverse paddle stroke, that is, everyone takes a backwards stroke with their paddles instead of a forward stroke.

The initial command should be "Stop Paddling" followed immediately by "Brace the Boat" if the boat is unstable and there is no immediate danger of a collision. If there is danger of a collision, the command, "Stop the Boat," should be given and the crew instructed by the helm to paddle backwards.

In a race situation when a collision is imminent, the helm must immediately tell the crew to "Stop the Boat." Failure by the crew to stop the boat in such circumstances will result in disqualification.

CAPSIZED OR SWAMPED DRAGON BOAT
≠ ≠

What to Do

In the event of a dragon boat capsizing or being swamped, each pair of paddlers should account for their buddies. The boat captain should immediately ensure that all the crew members are accounted for by instructing the crew to call out their numbers and noting the response. The crew must initially stay with the boat. When a boat has overturned (capsized), never swim underneath it. Leave it in the capsized position until instructed otherwise by the boat captain (see below concerning "Swamped Boat and Self Recovery").

A capsized boat can be used as a floating platform provided the crew members space themselves evenly around both sides of the boat, the boat captain having ensured that all "buddy pairs and threes" are accounted for. Even a boat, made to IDBF specifications, that has rolled completely and is fully swamped, will float and remain stable if the crew members space themselves evenly around the boat gunwales.

The boat captain must remain in control of the crew at all times and first ensure that all the crew members are accounted for as described above.

In a Race Situation

Await the arrival of the rescue boats. Crew members should attempt to retrieve them if their paddles are within easy reach. On the arrival of the rescue boats, the crew should move as directed by the operators of the boats, with the boat captain remaining *with the boat* until all members of the crew have been rescued.

If there are insufficient boats to rescue all the crew in one go and the water conditions are kind, or it is shallow, then, if the boat is capsized, up to six crew members can remain with the boat and start to "swim it" to the nearest shore.

This should only be done under the boat captain's control and when the swimmers are capable and not at risk. After the crew is safe, a rescue boat may be used to recover the dragon boat. (In cold water conditions, while awaiting rescue, crew members should, when holding onto the boat, try to conserve body heat by curling their legs up toward their chests and remaining as still and as calm as possible.)

Unescorted Crews

Should a rescue boat NOT be available then in calm conditions, the crew may attempt to "swim" a capsized boat to the nearest safe landing point, as directed by the boat captain. If conditions are not suitable for easily "swimming" the boat over a short distance, then under the instructions of the boat captain, it is recommended that the boat be rolled back to the upright position. Self-recovery can then be attempted.

Swamped Boat and Self-Recovery

With the crew members evenly spaced around the boat's gunwales, a swamped boat will support the crew. The boat is partially bailed out, using hands, paddles, and any other suitable implements available, e.g., boat bailers, until all the crew can re-enter the boat to complete the bailing and paddle the boat to the shore. One of the lightest crew members should re-enter the boat first and start the bailing process. A second person should then re-enter the boat and help with the bailing. As the water level in the boat goes down, more people should re-enter the boat and join the bailing process, until all the crew members are back in the boat and it can be paddled back to shore, without further risk of a capsize.

If self-recovery of the boat is not possible, then as a last resort, the crew may leave the boat and swim to shore in pairs, using the buddy system, again under the control of the boat captain. As with other methods, the crew must be accounted for at all times during any attempts to swim the boat or swim in pairs under the buddy system.

However, in a training situation crew members are advised to not attempt to swim to shore unless they are wearing PFAs. Should there be no alternative but to swim to the shore, then any crew member who is not wearing a PFA should join a buddy pair with PFAs, or make up groups of three, to provide mutual support and assistance during the swim.

Recovery of Craft

As soon as the boat is alongside the water's edge, the crew must again be accounted for on the land and any injuries dealt with immediately. If upturned, the boat may then be turned the right way up (in the water) and bailing commenced. The boat SHOULD NOT be dragged out of the water unless there is only a small amount of water left in it, as this puts considerable strain on the hull of the boat. Once the boat is almost empty of water, it can be lifted onto the bank and checked for damage and an account of all the boat's equipment.

Practice Drills

It is recommended that crews training regularly together should be introduced to at least one controlled capsize and an unescorted recovery exercise at an early stage in their training and then annually. This practice drill should be set up carefully, taking into account the time of year, and the weather and water conditions. During such drills in cold and/or deep water conditions, all crew members must wear PFAs, irrespective of their competitive experience, general physical fitness or swimming ability, and a rescue boat should be on standby. The wearing of PFAs may be relaxed at the crew captain's discretion in warm water conditions — for example, summer in a Mediterranean climate and where the water is less than 2.5 metres in depth.

CONCLUSION

Safety is the concern of every crew member and is largely a matter of common sense — USE IT! The overall responsibility for the crew off the water is the crew manager's and on the water is the boat captain's.

It is every competitor and official's responsibility to ensure that dragon boat racing is conducted as safely as possible.

SOURCES

International Dragon Boat Federation. *International Dragon Boat Federation Members Handbook*, 5th ed. 2008.

International Dragon Boat Federation. *Safety Standing Procedures for Dragon Boat Clubs and Crews When Training: Appendix 4 to the Water Safety Procedures.* 2007.

International Dragon Boat Federation. *Safety Procedures for Event Organizers of Festival and Sports Racing Regattas: Appendix to IDBF Water Safety Policy.* 2007.

14

龙　Riding the Dragon　船

Eleanor Nielsen

Photograph by Jan Oakley

Early Canadian Survivor teams, established in Vancouver, Toronto, and Montreal, first raced against each other at the Toronto International Dragon Boat Festival in 1998.

Women's teams dressed in pink are a common sight at dragon boat festivals these days, but it wasn't always so. The breast cancer dragon boat movement began in 1996 as a result of a small research study by Dr. Don McKenzie, a sports medicine specialist at the University of British Columbia, Vancouver. He questioned the logic behind the activity restrictions that were given to one of his patients with breast cancer. At that time, common practice was for doctors to advise women not to engage in strenuous and repetitive upper-body exercises after surgical node dissection and radiation therapy for fear of lymphedema, a debilitating swelling of the arm after lymph nodes are removed. Subsequent research confirmed that paddling does not increase the risk of this side effect.

Dr. McKenzie tested his theory by recruiting 22 women, post–breast cancer treatment, to make up a dragon boat crew. Carefully monitored, they trained for

I was told that "breast cancer had not only come back for a fourth time, but it had metastasized" to both of my lungs. Being "stage four" left me really scared for the first time, and very angry, as I feared that I would soon be leaving my children, my family and the world without ever making my "mark." I decided that as soon as I was well enough, I would do everything possible to fight breast cancer, and raise awareness in whatever way I could. I joined my team in November 2006, and it was the single most important (and knowingly selfish) decision of my whole cancer journey. Not only do I feel stronger physically, but also mentally, as I raise awareness that there is life after breast cancer. These beautiful women of all ages, shapes and sizes, support me like a sister, accept me as a friend and challenge me to be my best. Together, in perfect harmony we reach forward; delving deeper, accelerating in power and strength as we conquer our beasts and befriend our dragon by giving him wings, and making us fly.

— Breast Cancer Survivor

six months and were launched onto the unsuspecting dragon boat community for the first time at the 1996 Alcan Dragon Boat Festival in Vancouver. None of the women developed lymphedema but there was an additional, unexpected outcome. The original 22 refused to stop paddling and set about organizing the structure required to continue their team, Abreast In A Boat (AIAB). Through word of mouth and media, news of this unique activity spread across Canada. By the following year, breast cancer dragon boat teams were sprouting up in several other centres — Winnipeg, Toronto, Peterborough, Montreal, to name a few.

Some teams were fortunate to be located where dragon boating was well-established. Others were the first dragon boat team in their community. They had to fundraise to purchase boats as well as make the arrangements for coaching and practices. Breast cancer dragon boating quickly became a movement, starting in Canada, and gradually spreading into the United States, Australia, and New Zealand in the late 1990s. In recent years, two teams, Dragon Abreast — Brave Hearts (Australia) and the Avalon Team (Newfoundland) — have built their own dragon boats.

Photograph by Heather Maclaren

The Flower Ceremony, never failing to move those who are watching, has become part of regattas where Survivor teams race. Boats assemble at the False Creek Women's Regatta in Vancouver, British Columbia.

For many team members, dragon boating is their first team experience. The average age of members is 50, considerably older than most other teams, with a range of 28 to 80 years of age. Reflective of breast cancer statistics, the vast majority of paddlers are women, augmented by a small number of men.

Most teams share a common purpose of raising awareness of breast cancer and life after breast cancer, and encouraging an active life and the benefits that follow. Research has concluded that a physically active life decreases the risk of breast cancer. Putting a positive face on a devastating diagnosis is one outcome that dragon boating has enabled teams to do. The shared experience of facing breast cancer in its many varied forms creates what has been called, among team members, a "silent knowing" that helps to bind members together. The joy, camaraderie, and renewed energy they find in taking on this

Photograph by Jan Oakley

Friends and family, standing on shore, throw pink flowers into the water in memory of paddlers who have lost their fight against breast cancer. Pink, the colour commonly associated with breast cancer awareness, was launched in a 1992 Breast Cancer Awareness issue of *Self* magazine, attributed for the birth of the pink ribbon.

challenging team sport all help in the recovery and rehabilitation process.

A secondary benefit is support for team members facing rediagnosis or metastasis, the spread of cancer to other parts of the body. Breast cancer dragon boating provides an uncommon support format in that the primary purpose in coming together is sport, not support. With an insidious disease, like breast

> One of the greatest gifts I have got from dragon boating is the privilege of witnessing teammates as they live life fully to the end.
>
> — Breast Cancer Survivor

cancer, the sad reality is that all teams face death among their members. As Dr. McKenzie reported at a conference in 1999, if there are 10 teams, it is Lane 11, or breast cancer, that the paddlers are really racing against. Since then, the term "Lane 11" has come to be used to describe fighting breast cancer.

In recognition of this sad reality, the Flower Ceremony came into being. At the conclusion of Breast Cancer Challenges at dragon boat festivals around the world, breast cancer teams raft together on the water to share a moment of silence in honour of those who have lost the battle or are currently fighting it. Each paddler holds a pink flower. On signal, arms are raised and the flowers are tossed into the water, a powerful reminder that, although many survivors are well, living full and active lives, too many are still lost to breast cancer each year.

In 1998, breast cancer teams were invited, for the first time, to participate in the IDBF World Club Crew Championships in Wellington, New Zealand, followed by subsequent invitations to Rome, Italy; Poznan, Poland; and Cape Town, South Africa. At each of these venues, advocates returned home full of enthusiasm for bringing breast cancer dragon boating to their countries. Throughout these years, Abreast In A Boat provided guidance and assistance under the capable and gentle hands of Sandy Smith who held the AIAB position of Global Liaison.

Besides raising awareness, many teams have assumed fundraising goals for breast cancer services at local hospitals, cancer support organizations, breast cancer research, and other badly needed services.

In 2001, the first team of Internationally Abreast came together at the Toronto International Dragon Boat Race Festival with members from different teams in Canada, as well as six paddlers from Australia. In 2004, three crews, made up of paddlers from Canada, the United States, Australia, and New Zealand, met for the first time in Shanghai and raced during the 5th IDBF World Championships. Internationally Abreast aptly demonstrates the universal nature of breast cancer. At this event, participation of the first Chinese breast cancer dragon boat team, along with the Singapore team, confirmed the appeal of dragon boating for women around the world.

In 2008, there are about 160 teams worldwide. The majority are still in Canada with about 55, closely followed by Australia at 43. Along with the United States and New Zealand, there are teams in the United Kingdom, Italy, Poland, Czech Republic, Singapore, China, South Africa, Malaysia, and Hong Kong. There have been three international breast cancer events. Two of these, Vancouver in 2005 and Australia in 2007, were participatory and the third, Singapore in 2006, was competitive. At the Australian event, Abreast in Australia, there were 70 teams. It was a joyous spectacle to behold. The participatory events are run on IDBF rules but all crew members, including steers, must be diagnosed with breast cancer. Competition is natural, but the main focus is participation and everyone receives a medal.

An umbrella organization, the International Breast Cancer Paddling Commission (IBCPC), was approved by teams attending the Abreast in Australia and is now overseeing plans for the third International IBCPC Participatory Festival in 2010.

A research study was conducted in the early 2000s with 408 Ontario paddlers from 13 teams responding to a survey and 60 participating in interviews. It confirmed the perception that breast cancer dragon boat paddlers as a group are living their lives to the fullest, promoting personal wellness and public awareness while giving new meaning to the term survivorship.

When Dr. McKenzie embarked on that small research project in 1996, neither he nor the volunteers making up that first team could have predicted the lure of the dragon and dragon boating to thousands of women living with breast cancer.

SOURCES

McKenzie, Donald C. "Abreast In A Boat: A Race against Breast Cancer." *Canadian Medical Association Journal*, Vol. 159 (August 1998), 376–378.

Mitchell, Terry, et al. "Survivor Dragon Boating: A Vehicle to Reclaim and Enhance Life After Treatment for Breast Cancer." *Health Care for Women International*, Vol. 28 (February 2007), 122–140.

15

The Little Team That Grew

Kathy Levy

龙　船

When Kathy Levy, founder of Knot A Breast, could no longer paddle because of injury, she transferred her passion to steering. Here, she is at the helm for a crew during the GWN Spring Training Camp in Melbourne, Florida.

Courtesy of Kathy Levy

We walk along so many different paths in our lifetime. Some we walk by choice. Others are thrust upon us, not of our choosing. In that instance it is up to the individual to make of the path what they can. One such path would be the diagnosis of breast cancer. If during that time or the subsequent treatment period, someone had suggested to me that my future would include a dragon boat, many practices on the water, and hours working out at a gym, I might have wondered at such an imagination. I might have hoped but never would I have been able to claim this vision as mine. So how does breast cancer and dragon boating end up on the same page, paragraph and line?

Dr. Don McKenzie was determined to get women out from under the fear of living with breast cancer and to get them moving on a different and exciting path. In 1997, I learned of his intention. He had done his homework. I did mine. In the summer of 1998 I put together Knot A Breast, Hamilton's breast cancer survivors' dragon boat team. The first race was, of course, in Hamilton. The rest is part of history. The team started to grow, practised hard, and enjoyed learning as the years rolled by … all 10 of them!

The team is made up of as many varied interests and personalities as there are faces. On the boat, one common interest binds everyone tightly. They have each waged a battle with breast cancer and they are here to fight back, paddle, give support to others, laugh, and deliver a message. The message is simple. They want to tell others, just diagnosed, that, indeed, there is life after breast cancer. Life may not be as perfect as originally planned but it can still be so very worthwhile, inspiring, and a boat load of fun!

As a crew of paddlers, we have experienced thrilling highs. As a team of breast cancer warriors, we have felt soul-deep losses. Sports teams usually do not have to face the passing away of their members over a season, but out of our lives have gone many a treasured soul and paddling mate. Each of our friends, to whom we have had to say a final farewell, is on the boat with us. They live on in our memories and in our hearts as we carry them over the water and into the wind. They inspire us to dig deeper, fight harder, and paddle stronger. They are a part of us and we will never forget them.

Our team started to make the change from a breast cancer team to a competitive team in 2003. We paddled our way to the next level of dragon boating by way of a letter I sent to Jim Farintosh:

Hi Jim,

As per our conversation, I have a number of women coming to the upcoming winter training camp, we would like to be split into two groups.

Photograph by Laurie Wierzbicki

Members of Busting Out, based in Ottawa, Ontario, participate in the Flower Ceremony at the Ottawa festival. Losing teammates is a reality that Survivor teams face every season.

Hopefully, at some point during the training camp, we will be able to come together as a group to practise what we have learned from different style coaching.

Knot A Breast approaches paddling aggressively. We want to improve our technique and our endurance. We push ourselves beyond our limits and we enjoy it. We want to compete ably beside "normal" paddlers as we have started to do this past season. So we would like to have coaches that will push us and keep pushing us.

Thanks again for helping me out.

Kathy

This is when Knot A Breast started pushing the envelope … from a breast cancer dragon boat team to a competitive dragon boat team!

Encouragement of the group as a whole and of the individual plays a big part on this team. One member, afraid of water before cancer, has become a triathlete and can swim miles at a time. The team has cultivated entrepreneurs and helped to launch a few businesses that just needed some encouragement. With that same encouragement, some on the team have gone into the community to educate and inform the public and to deliver our message. Four of us were also crew members of the first Canadian National Grand Masters dragon boat team. Don't count us out because we have had breast cancer. We are here, ready and able to put our own twist on this journey and ride the dragon our way. And so we paddle!

Practising begins in January at a pool. Learning the correct technique of the paddle stroke is worked on and developed through to April. The members also commit to a routine of physical workouts at least twice a week to prepare themselves for late spring when they finally get into the boat on Hamilton Bay. That is an event they all look forward to with keen anticipation. What a feeling of accomplishment to be boarding the boat and leaving the pool behind for the season. Paddling practices are held twice a week throughout the summer months. The Knot A Breast dragon boats can easily be seen from the shoreline at Pier 4 in Hamilton. In wind, rain, or sun, the team continues to paddle, perfecting that stroke and enjoying the freedom of the ride. To move a 680 kilogram boat, plus the weight of the 22 occupants, is no easy task. To say it is gruelling and takes a certain amount of stamina is not an exaggeration. And so there is dedication, drive, commitment, and sheer will power on that boat and, did I mention, fun! Our focus in the boat is on stroke mechanics and proper timing. This becomes so all-encompassing. We leave our breast cancer on shore and become athletes and competitors on the water. We concentrate on digging, rotating, reaching, using our legs, pulling back, and giving all our strength to each and every paddle stroke. The quest is to do our best and we come away from every race with something to improve, repeat, change, grow, and win.

In a race, we compete against the clock with whomever happens to be placed in the same heat. By the way, Knot A Breast does well! Those other teams often consist of young, healthy and strong men and women who train to win and make their supporters proud. Into that fray goes Knot A Breast. Being recognized as "athletes" is most important to us. We have worked hard for this title for many years. We revel in competing against able-bodied teams. And they notice us. An email from a competitor says it all:

Hi Pat, Alex, Kathy,

I was overwhelmed by the weekend but more so by the BCS [Breast Cancer Survivor] teams. I have come to realize the dynamics at play that impact us all in a way that brings out the best whether this be Premier or Grand Master. But I think it's teams such as your own that show us all the value of belonging and competing with the best while being recognized as trained athletes in our own right. Congratulations to all. Hail to the Champions.

Reg Landry

Team Captain, Cascades Grand Masters

All are determined to never give up and never give in ... their creed and motto.

At each race event, there is a Breast Cancer Challenge for breast cancer teams. An emotional race unfolds as we are well aware of each other, what brought each of us to the starting line, the battle we have all waged, the race we are in every day of our lives, and the finish line yet to be crossed.

Every season has its share of thrilling and memorable races and achievements but most notable is a 2005 international event that took place in Welland, Ontario. Knot A Breast had been invited to compete with the cream of the crop of dragon boaters including 12 other breast cancer dragon boat teams from North America. After the Breast Cancer Challenge, Knot A Breast proudly took home the gold. However, another race still loomed! It was our first 2,000-metre race ever! Races are usually 500 metres long. The 13 breast cancer teams would meet again, but this time instead of the boats lining up abreast, each one would approach the starting line 15 seconds apart. Since we had won the Breast Cancer Challenge, we were last to approach the starting line. You could feel the collective heart beat on the boat. There was no other sound! The starter's pistol rang and we were off. On the back 500 metres, we passed an American team from Philadelphia, a well-respected competitor. Some moments after the race, it was announced over the loudspeaker that the "premier women's breast cancer dragon boat team in North America" was none other than Hamilton's Knot A Breast. We had won our first 2,000-metre race. Did our hearts soar? You bet!

On Saturday, June 24, 2006, Knot A Breast was competing along with 192 other teams in Ottawa at the biggest dragon boat race in North America. At the end of the day, Knot A Breast had won the Breast Cancer Challenge with times that qualified the crew to be invited to return and compete the next day. No other breast cancer team had qualified. On Sunday, Knot A Breast was representing not only Hamilton but all the other breast cancer teams by competing with the best of the best. At the end of the weekend, Knot A Breast was informed that they had placed in the top third of all teams, 62 out of 192, and 14 out of the 42 highly skilled and competitive women's teams. All of those other crews were "healthy" teams. Did our souls soar? You bet! Nine years ago, Knot A Breast was happy just to finish a race. That is now a memory, a starting point, so to speak. But every team has to have a starting point.

We will each cross that finish line one day leaving behind a time full of memories, tears, fears, laughter, hugs, caring, supporting, poems, stories, friends, family, and supporters. Yes, we were dealt an unexpected hand to play and, yes, we are playing it well. The crew is a support team on land and a competitive and athletic team of warriors on the water. As one paddler stated in an email:

Subject: tonight's high

yo, Kathy, the power and drive that you felt tonight is the direct result of your continuous drive, determination, spirit (that you have enkindled in so many of us), loyalty, patience, encouragement, enthusiasm, direction, inspiration, and stick-to-it-tiveness, through the good, the bad, and the ugly ... you have created what you felt out there tonight ... I am so very proud to be part of it and never does a day go by that I don't say a big thank you to the Power that directed me to Knot A Breast. See you at the game.

With a hug,
Margaretanne

And in another email:

Subject: Paddling
Chair, Tampa Dragon Boat Festival

Hi Kevin,
Can you hook up Sarasota [Florida] with Kathy? She's been in the game a long time and could provide valuable advice and direction particularly with starting a Breast Cancer Team. Kathy manages one of the best (fastest) BCS clubs on the continent. They were 2005 NACCC gold medallists.

Mike [Kerkmann, GWN]

Photograph by Jan Oakley

The average age of Survivor team members is generally higher than those of most other teams. Undeterred, these crews race full out down the course.

As part of our winter training this past year, we added two evenings dedicated to learning more about our nutritional needs and other health and wellness issues. The average age on our team is 55. We will do whatever it takes to stay in the competitive realm of dragon boating.

Twenty paddlers, a coach, a steersperson, one heart, one mind, one stroke — that defines Knot A Breast, a premier breast cancer dragon boat team. As we head into our 11th season, Knot A Breast will continue to challenge ourselves and other teams, both breast cancer and corporate alike, and raise the bar in competition. We strive to accomplish our quest, which is "to do our best."

And we paddle on!

16

Canada and the International Scene

龙　船

Matt Smith

> My son was a boy who never liked sports … But, being a caring parent, I persisted until I found a sport that he liked — dragon boating. And how he loved it!
>
> This season, his dragon boating team offered a free paddle for new paddlers. Now I paddle too.
> — Loretta Hughes, Chilliwack, British Columbia

Dragon boats first arrived in Canada in 1986. While the history of dragon boating here may be short, relative to the thousands of years it has existed in China, there has been an explosion in popularity and not a dull moment has passed since.

The responsibility for the governance of dragon boating falls to the International Dragon Boat Federation and Dragon Boat Canada, the Canadian member. As the sport grew in popularity, so did the need for standardized rules and championship races. And so, these organizations were born.

In the Beginning, Before 1991
≠ ≠

The IDBF considers the modern era of dragon boat racing to have begun in Hong Kong when the first international races were held in 1976. In fact, until the IDBF began organizing international races, the annual Hong Kong race was considered the unofficial club crew world championship of dragon boating and, to this day, remains one of the largest events in the world and the spiritual capital of the sport.

Throughout the 1970s and 1980s, the sport spread through Europe and into North America.

The boats were introduced to Canada at Expo 86 in Vancouver as part of the Chinese exposition. After a few local crews got a taste of dragon boating, the sport took off and has not looked back. Not long afterward, Canada's two oldest festivals in Vancouver and Toronto were hosts to hundreds of crews and thousands of participants.

The Formation of IDBF and DBRCC, 1991–1999
≠ ≠

In 1991 a handful of nations, led by the godfather of modern dragon boating, Mike Haslam of the United Kingdom, came together and formed the IDBF. Canada soon followed in 1993 with the creation of its own national federation, called the Dragon Boat Racing Council of Canada (DBRCC). The organization was set up by Adrian Lee with the support of the Vancouver and Toronto festivals that, to this day, remain the founding and permanent festival members of what was later renamed Dragon Boat Canada.

Throughout the 1990s, the IDBF's prominence and membership gradually grew. In 1995, it hosted the first World Championship event in Yueyang, China, followed by the first World Club Crew Championship in Vancouver, Canada, in 1996. During this period, the DBRCC did not play a large role in Canada; however, everything would suddenly change in the year 2000.

GROWTH, EXCITEMENT, AND TURBULENCE, 1999–2006

≠ ≩

Up until 2000, the world championships did not garner much attention outside of Toronto and Vancouver, these two areas represented by the Greater Toronto Dragon Boat Club (GTDBC) and False Creek Racing Canoe Club (FCRCC) respectively. Both organizations had an agreement whereby the GTDBC would supply the open crew and FCRCC, the mixed and women's crews, at the world championship. This arrangement changed in 2000, the year before the 2001 IDBF World Championship in Philadelphia, when the GTDBC decided to challenge FCRCC for the women's and mixed entries as well. A race was organized at the Vancouver dragon boat festival; GTDBC won the mixed entry with the FCRCC successfully defending the women's title. This event marked an important turning point in the history of the DBRCC. Suddenly, this small organization was going to be called upon to settle who was going to be representing Canada at the world championships. Coupled with this turn of events was a growing interest in the Club Crew World Championships, which, at the time, were limited to three entries per country. DBRCC needed a way to determine which crews would race at these events as well.

During this time, the organization was re-constituted and re-named into the more broadly-represented Dragon Boat Canada/Bateau-Dragon Canada. The organization was separated into three administrative regions — East, West, and Central. Each had three directors who together made up the board of nine members. An executive committee, which included a secretary, treasurer, and president, was responsible for overseeing the day-to-day administration.

Interest in dragon boat "sport" soared. For national team trials, two crews took part in 2000, three in 2002, and 28 in 2004. As one can imagine, with that many people fighting for a piece of the action, there was never a dull day for volunteer-run DBC. Add to this mix the plethora of community, festival, and corporate groups that were also interested in dragon boating. At times, the situation threatened to rip the organization apart.

By 2006, things began to stabilize and it was during this year that DBC received what could be best described as a gift from the gods. The Ontario Trillium Foundation, which redistributes lottery money to non-profit organizations, recognized the popularity of the sport and acknowledged that the DBC could benefit from its help. The foundation awarded DBC a $250,000 grant over three years to develop domestic programs and, more important, hire full-time staff.

During this entire period, the IDBF was going through its own successes and trials. Participation at its championship events was soaring, but its governance was being challenged by the International Canoe Federation (ICF), which, upon seeing the popularity of dragon boating, decided to claim dragon boating as one of its own disciplines. While the ICF and IDBF enjoyed a cordial relationship in the 1990s, things changed in 1999 when the ICF came under new leadership, and further encouraged all of its national sport organization members to do the same.

Matters came to a head when the ICF began blocking the IDBF's membership application to the General Association of International Sport Federations (GAISF). GAISF is an affiliate of the International Olympic Committee that oversees all sports, both Olympic and non-Olympic. The debate was finally settled in 2007 when the IDBF won its greatest victory to date. The IDBF was voted in as a member. This recognition acknowledged the sport of dragon boating as unique and placed it, alongside and on equal ground, with other recognized sports, like sailing, rowing, and canoeing.

Canada was not immune to the governance debate although matters never escalated to the extent they did internationally. Following the direction of the ICF, Canoe Kayak Canada (CKC) has shown interest in dragon boating, but mostly as a development tool for its flatwater racing programs and as a fundraiser for its canoe clubs. Meanwhile DBC seeks to support dragon boaters throughout their dragon boating careers, and to support, not only elite racing, but the community organizations, corporate entities, and charities that all take part in the sport. The CKC/DBC relationship could best be described as a work in progress, but there is strong support from both memberships for co-operation.

Photograph by Jens Ronneberger

Telek Bahang Dam in Penang, Malaysia, was the site of the 2008 Club Crew World Championships. Club crews from Canada dominated, particularly in the Premier and Senior Divisions.

2007 TO PRESENT
≠ ≒

With recognition of the sport and the support of full-time administration, the DBC and IDBF have never been better. Although many challenges and issues from the early 2000s are yet to be overcome, both the sport and the organizations that run it show a promising future.

CHAMPIONSHIP RACES
≠ ≒

The IDBF hosts several types of championship races

Photograph by Jan Oakley

Canadian Premier Women proudly wave the flag while taking a victory lap at the 2007 World Dragon Boat Racing Championships in Sydney, Australia.

at which Canada has enjoyed tremendous success. These include the IDBF World Championships, World Club Crew Championships, and World Corporate/Community Championships.

World Championships

The pinnacle of dragon boating, the IDBF World Championships are held every two years on odd years. To date, world championships have been scheduled at the following locations:

- 1995 — Yueyang, China;
- 1997 — Hong Kong, China;
- 1999 — Nottingham, England;
- 2001 — Philadelphia, Pennsylvania;
- 2003 — Poznan, Poland;[1]

Photograph by Normand Beaulieu

The Canadian Senior Open Crew lines up in the marshalling tent at the 2007 World Dragon Boat Racing Championships in Sydney, Australia.

- 2004 — Shanghai, China;
- 2005 — Berlin, Germany;
- 2007 — Sydney, Australia;
- 2009 — Prague, Czech Republic;
- 2011 — Tampa, Florida.

Canada has had tremendous success at the world championships. For an incredible run, Canada was the Nations Cup winner at the 2001, 2003, and 2004 world championships. The Nations Cup is awarded to the country that best performs in the Premier Division. In 2005 and 2007, while

Photograph by Normand Beaulieu

Another gold medal for Canada. The scoreboard shows the results of the 200-metre Senior Mixed Final in Sydney, Australia, 2007.

Canada did not win the Nations Cup, placing 3rd and 2nd respectively, Canadian crews won more medals than any other country across all divisions (Junior, Premier, Senior, and Grand Dragon) with particular dominance in the Senior and Grand Dragon Divisions.

In Canada, qualification for a world championship race is determined for each particular program at the Canadian National Team Trials that are held the year before the race. The winning program then becomes "Team Canada" and has the right to put together the crew for the competition.

3rd WDBRC Nottingham, England 1999				
	250 m	500 m	1000 m	2000 m
Junior Open	No entry	No entry	No entry	
Junior Women				
Junior Mixed	No entry	No entry	No entry	
Premier Open	6th	Bronze	Silver	
Premier Women	Silver	Bronze	Silver	
Premier Mixed	Silver	5th		
Senior Open	5th	5th		
Senior Women				
Senior Mixed	Bronze	Bronze		

4th WDBRC Philadelphia, U.S. 2001				
	250 m	500 m	1000 m	2000 m
Junior Open	No entry	No entry	No entry	
Junior Women	No entry	No entry		
Junior Mixed	Silver	Results not available		
Premier Open	Gold	Gold	Gold	
Premier Women	Silver	Results not available	Bronze	
Premier Mixed	Gold	Gold		
Senior Open	Canada A – Gold Canada B – 4th	Canada A – Silver Canada B – Bronze	Canada A – Gold Canada B – Bronze	
Senior Women	Silver	Silver		

Senior Mixed	Canada B – 4th Canada A – 5th	Results not available		

World Nations Cup Poznan, Poland 2003				
	250 m	500 m	1000 m	2000 m
Junior Open	5th	Bronze	4th	
Junior Women				
Junior Mixed	Bronze	Silver		
Premier Open	5th	5th	Gold	
Premier Women	Gold	Bronze	Silver	
Premier Mixed	Silver	Gold		
Senior Open	Canada A – Silver Canada B – Bronze	Canada A – Gold	Canada A – Silver Canada B – 5th	Bronze
Senior Women	Canada A – Bronze			5th
Senior Mixed	Canada B – Bronze Canada A – 4th	Canada B – Bronze Canada A – 5th		

5th WDBRC Shanghai, China 2004 (rescheduled)				
	200 m	500 m	1000 m	2000 m
Junior Open	Canada A – 4th	Canada A – 4th	Canada A – 4th	
Junior Women				
Junior Mixed	Canada A – Bronze			
Premier Open	Gold	Silver	Silver	

| Premier Women | Gold | 4th | Bronze | |
| Premier Mixed | 4th | Silver | | |

Senior Open	Gold	Bronze	Bronze	
Senior Women	Canada A – Silver Canada B – 7th	Canada A – Silver Canada B – 7th	Canada A – Gold	
Senior Mixed	Canada A – Silver Canada B – 4th	Canada A – Silver Canada B – 4th		

6th WDBRC Berlin, Germany 2005

	200 m	500 m	1000 m	2000 m
Junior Open	Silver	Silver	Silver	
Junior Women	Gold	Gold		
Junior Mixed	Canada A – Bronze Canada B – 4th	Canada A – Bronze Canada B – 4th		
Premier Open	Silver	Bronze		6th
Premier Women	Gold	Gold	Gold	
Premier Mixed	Silver	Silver		6th
Senior Open	Canada A – Silver Canada B – Bronze	Canada A – Silver Canada B – Bronze	Canada A – Silver Canada B – Bronze	
Senior Women	Canada A – Silver Canada B – Bronze	Canada A – Silver Canada B – Bronze	Canada A – Silver Canada B – Bronze	
Senior Mixed	Canada – Gold Canada – Bronze	Canada A – Silver Canada B – Bronze		

7th WDBRC Sydney, Australia 2007				
	200 m	500 m	1000 m	2000 m
Junior Open	Canada A – 4th Canada B – 5th	Canada A – 4th Canada B – 5th	Canada A – Bronze Canada B – 6th	Canada B – Silver Canada A – Bronze
Junior Women	Canada B – Gold Canada A – 6th	Canada B – Gold Canada A – Bronze		
Junior Mixed	Canada A – Silver Canada B – 5th	Canada A – Silver Canada B – Bronze		Canada B – Silver Canada A – Bronze
Premier Open			5th	5th
Premier Women	Gold	Gold	Gold	
Premier Mixed	4th	Silver		
Senior Open	Canada A – Gold	Canada A – Gold	Canada A – Gold	Canada A – Gold
Senior Women	Canada A – Gold Canada B – Silver	Canada A – Gold Canada B – Silver	Canada B – Bronze	
Senior Mixed	Canada A – Gold Canada B – Silver	Canada A –Gold Canada B – Silver		Canada A – Gold Canada B – Silver
Grand Dragon Open	Gold	Gold	Gold	Gold
Grand Dragon Women	Silver	Bronze		
Grand Dragon Mixed	Gold	Gold		Silver

Notes:
1. Results are not available for 1st WDBRC, Yueyang, China or 2nd WDBRC, Hong Kong.
2. Shaded area indicates that the Racing Class was not offered.

Photograph by Jens Ronneberger

The "dragons" rest at the race site in Penang, Malaysia, before 180 crews from around the world compete in the 2008 Club Crew World Championships.

Club Crew World Championships

The Club Crew World Championship (CCWC) has proven to be extremely popular in the world of dragon boating. The goal of the CCWC is to promote participation and recognize the strongest clubs in the world. Each country is allowed to send up to five entries per racing class, and the IDBF often uses the event to encourage racing where dragon boating is developing. With locations like New Zealand, Malaysia, and South Africa, and a wide diversity of participation, the CCWCs are always a colourful and memorable experience. CCWCs are held on even years, opposite world championships. They have been held in the following locations:

When I started dragon boating in 2003, I was overweight and out of shape. Within three years, I lost 40 pounds and had started strength and aerobic training. Being a Canadian National Champion in 2007 and 2008, and world champion in 2006 and 2008, is such an awesome feeling for someone over 50.

— Barb Michno, Toronto, Ontario

The 2006 Club Crew World Championships were held in Toronto, Ontario, on the newly built waterfront race course.

- 1996 — Vancouver, Canada;
- 1998 — Wellington, New Zealand;
- 2002 — Rome, Italy;
- 2004 — Cape Town, South Africa;
- 2006 — Toronto, Canada;
- 2008 — Penang, Malaysia.

The year 2006 is of particular note for Canadians. The CCWC that was held in Toronto was the most expensive one ever produced with a budget of $26 million, most of that for the construction of the racecourse at Marilyn Bell Park.

As with the world championships, Canadian club crews usually perform well at the CCWC. Like the world's, qualification for the CCWC takes place in the year before the event. Canadian crews must race a series of qualifying races with the final race-offs at the Canadian National Championships. Following the

Toronto CCWC, interest in the event has taken off and Canada generally boasts the largest contingent of any country. In 2008, Canada sent over 40 crews to Malaysia, 30 percent of the overall participation, to a nation on the other side of the planet! Canadian teams dominated the medal standings.

Other Championships

The IDBF has recently launched the World Corporate/Community Championships as a means of bringing the world's recreational paddlers together.

Photograph by Jan Oakley

The Canadian Senior Open crew members and friends celebrate a medal win in Sydney, Australia.

Still in its infancy, the championships have been held in Welland, Ontario (2007) and will next be held in Tampa, Florida (2011).

Both the European (EDBF) and Asian Dragon Boat Federations (ADBF) hold club crew and continental championships on opposite years to the IDBF's. North America has previously held club crew championships in 2003 and 2005, but with only two participating nations, the event has yet to prove a staple.

Championships have been, and may be held, for other groups as well, the most well known of which are the Breast Cancer Survivor Championships, held every two years.

Photograph by Jens Ronneberger

The Outer Harbour Senior Women win gold at the 2008 Club Crew Championships in Penang, Malaysia.

RACING IN CANADA

≠ ≯

Dragon boat racing in Canada can be described as nothing short of a phenomenon. What other sport sees firemen, breast cancer survivors, and Olympic athletes of all ages lined up against one another!

The roots of Canadian dragon boating lie within the Chinese communities and, since its arrival, the sport has been a hit with the corporate community. The large corporate and community base is one of the primary differences between Canada and other nations where dragon boating exists primarily as a club sport.

The 2006 CCWC in Toronto was a launch pad for club racing. The surge in interest for the event forced DBC and its members to organize themselves

Photograph by Susan Humphries

The joy of winning by the Canadian Senior Women in Sydney, Australia, is reflected in the faces of the athletes.

into a proper club system. In 2007 DBC held the first national championships in Calgary. The inaugural event was a partnership with the Calgary Dragon Boat Festival. In 2008, the event was held in Toronto as a stand-alone event for the first time with 40 crews. The national championships are held yearly and rotated through Canada's three administrative regions. The 2009 championships will be held in Montreal, and 2010 is planned for Harrison Hot Springs, British Columbia.

As time moves forward, club growth and interest in dragon boat "sport" is taking off. The coming

> I just love to watch all the "newbies" try the sport and "catch the paddling bug"! It's such a great sport, even my husband joined. He now sterns and coaches for us!
> — Brenda Pentland, London, Ontario

years will see the development of sport racing circuits, particularly in densely-populated areas, like southern Ontario and Quebec.

NOTES

1. Shanghai was originally scheduled for 2003 but was cancelled because of a SARS outbreak. Rather than cancelling the event, a decision was made to hold a special World Nations Cup in Poznan, Poland, and reschedule the World Championship in Shanghai the following year.

龙　Glossary　船

A

Aerobic: The physiological condition where energy is supplied by oxygen.

Anaerobic: The physiological condition where energy is supplied in the absence of oxygen.

B

Bailer: A scoop for bailing water from a boat.

Boat Helm: *See* Steersperson.

Bow: The front of a boat.

Buoy: A floating device that identifies a lane, turning point, finish, and start lines.

C

C-: A letter indicating *canoe*, followed by 1 for a single paddler, 2 for two paddlers, and so on.

Capsize: To turn over. Also referred to as *huli*, a Hawaiian term meaning to turn over or upside down.

Carbon Fibre: Synthetic, high-tech fibre used to construct lightweight paddles and boats.

Catch: The phase of the stroke when the paddle first comes in contact with the water.

Classes of Racing (ages 12 and over): *See* Grand Dragons, Junior, Mixed, Open, Premier, Senior, Under 23, *and* Women.

Club Crew World Championships (CCWC): Up to five different club crews from each IDBF member may compete in each competition class.

Connection: The resistance and feel of the water to maximize the power of the paddle blade.

Coxswain or Cox: *See* Steersperson.

Crew: The paddlers, steersperson, drummer, and other persons who may be on the boat. The crew will comprise one steersperson and one drummer and up to 20 paddlers.

Crosswind: Wind cutting diagonally across.

Current: Moving water.

D

Did Not Finish (DNF): Any crew not finishing a race for any reason, including disqualification, is labelled "Did Not Finish."

Disqualification (DQ): Disqualification when a race rule has been violated.

Drive: The phase of a stroke when the paddle is pulled through the water.

Drummer: The person who sits at the front and drums.

E

Elite: A classification for paddlers at a world-class

level where crews are selected from a pool of national candidates and funded by government or a parent organization.

Engine Room: The middle seats of paddlers.

Ergometer or Erg: A rowing machine used for off-water workouts and quantitative measurement of a paddler's strength.

Exit: The end of the stroke's drive when the paddle blade leaves the water.

F

False Start: A start that a crew unfairly initiates before the starting command. A second horn or other signal signifies a false start and may result in disqualification.

Festival: An individual, corporation, or unincorporated organization owning or organizing a dragon boat festival or racing event.

Finish: The point near the end of a race when the team stroke rate and power is increased.

Flag Puller: The crew member who grabs the flag at the finish line to show that the boat has finished a race. This tradition is popular in Taiwanese dragon boat races.

Flatwater: Conditions that provide calm water, as opposed to whitewater.

Foot Brace: A support against which paddlers brace

their feet and add effectiveness to their paddle stroke.

G

Grand Dragons Class: An age group under the Senior Racing Class. Racers must be 50 or over by June 1 in the year of competition.

Gunwale: The top edge of the boat's sides.

H

Headwind: Wind coming from straight ahead.

Heats: Qualifying races to set the divisions and to determine the winners.

Helm: *See* Steersperson.

Huli: *See* Capsize.

J

Junior Class: Racers must be 12 or over and under 18, except the steersperson.

K

K-: A letter indicating *kayak*, followed by 1 for a single paddler, 2 for two paddlers, and so on.

L

Loading Area: The location where boats are loaded and unloaded.

M

Mixed Class: Crews must have a minimum of eight and a maximum of 12 female paddlers.

O

OC-: A letter indicating *outrigger canoe*, followed by 1 for a single paddler, 2 for two paddlers, and so on.

Open Class: There are no restrictions on crew composition.

Overtaking: To move past another boat.

P

Pacers: The paddlers at the front of the boat. Also referred to as the "strokes."

Palm Grip: The handle on top of a paddle.

Personal Flotation Aid (PFA): A life jacket or vest.

Photo Finish: A race in which the leading boats cross the finish line so close together that the winners must be determined by a photograph taken at the moment of crossing.

Premier Class: No age restrictions.

Pull: The phase of the stroke when the paddle is buried in the water and is pulled back.

R

Racing Classes: *See* Classes of Racing.

Rate: The pace of paddling or the number of paddle strokes per minute.

Reach: The maximum extension of the stroke before the paddle hits the water.

Recovery: The final phase of the stroke when the paddle is snapped forward to the catch position.

Referee: The race official who has control of the race before the start. Only a steersperson or drummer may communicate with the referee.

Regatta: A series of races, involving several different classes of men, women, and youth up to elite levels.

Rockets: The paddlers at the back of the boat. Also known as "turbo" or "back six."

Rotation: The torso rotation to maximize the reach or extension of the stroke.

Rushing: The timing of paddling in the boat is ahead or out of synchronization.

S

Senior Class: Racers must be 40 or over by June 1 in the year of competition. This includes the steersperson, but not the drummer.

Series: A race strategy when the crew increases intensity and/or stroke rate for 10 to 20 strokes.

Sprint: Occurs when a crew raises the rate and drives hard at the start or the finish of a race.

Starter: The race official who has control of the start once the referee passes on control. The starter asks crews to advance to, but not over, the start line.

Steersperson: The person who steers a boat with the steering oar and encourages the crew. Also known as the "coxswain," "cox," "steerer," "helm," "boat helm," or "sweep."

Stern: The rear of the boat.

Stroke: The action of moving a paddle into, through, and out of the water.

Stroke Rate: The paddling pace or number of times the paddle goes through the water per minute.

Strokes: *See* Pacers.

Swamp: To fill a boat with water.

Sweep: *See* Steersperson.

T

T-Grip: The handle on top of a paddle.

Tailwind: Wind coming from behind.

Turbo: *See* Rockets.

U

Under-23 Class: Racers must be over 17 and under 23.

W

Wake: The temporary trail in the water behind the boat. Also called the wash.

Wash Riding: A boat manoeuvre in which the steersperson positions the boat on the wake of a leading boat and, at a strategic moment, drops off the wake to sprint ahead. Also known as "wake riding" or "wash hanging."

Women: Racing class for all female crews, including drummer and steersperson.

World Corporate and Community Championships (Corcom): New and experienced crews representing businesses and the community at large from IDBF members or affiliates may compete. There are no restrictions on numbers.

World Dragon Boat Racing Championships (WDBRC): One representative crew per nation or territory can compete in each competition class. For Junior racing divisions, two crews per competition class are allowed.

龙　Boat Commands　船

Attention Please: Prepare for the first stroke at the race start. The start signal occurs within 10 seconds. Also known as "Paddles Up."

Back It Down: Paddle backward to reverse the boat. Also known as "Back Paddle."

Brace the Boat: Extend the paddle blade flat on the water's surface to stabilize the boat.

Check the Boat: Stop the boat from moving forward or backward.

Draw Strokes Left: Lean out to the left side and pull directly toward the boat to move it sideways. Also known as "Draw Left."

Draw Strokes Right: Lean out to the right side and pull directly toward the boat to move it sideways. Also known as "Draw Right."

Easy All or Let It Run: Stop paddling and let boat coast.

Feather: Place the paddle horizontal with flat blade resting on top of the water and move paddles back and forth as if they are buttering the water's surface. This movement stabilizes the boat when at rest on choppy water conditions or when paddlers are changing seats in the boat.

Go: Begin paddling.

Hard Up Against the Side: Sit with the hip pressed against the gunwale.

Hold the Boat: Place paddles in the water to stop or slow the boat.

Let It Run: Stop paddling and let boat coast. Also known as "Easy All" or "All Down."

Paddles Up: Position paddle ready to enter the water for the first stroke. Also known as "All Up."

Paddles Buried: Bury paddle blade in the water, ready for the first stroke of the start.

Pry Stroke Left: Lean out to the left side and push directly away from the boat to move it sideways. Also known as "Left Pry."

Pry Stroke Right: Lean out to the right side and push directly away from the boat to move it sideways. Also known as "Right Pry."

Push Off Left: Push the boat away from the dock or whatever is on the left side of the boat.

Push Off Right: Push the boat away from the dock or whatever is on the right side of the boat.

Push Strokes Left: Push out to the left, perpendicular to the boat.

Push Strokes Right: Push out to the right, perpendicular to the boat.

Rudder the Boat: Place paddle blades vertically in the water up tight against the gunwale to stop the boat from drifting at the start line.

Ready Ready: Command in race start to position for first stroke with paddles buried or tips out of the water.

Series: A combination of 10 to 20 strokes that is quicker and/or more forceful during a race.

Sit Up: Cue for all paddlers to focus and listen for next voice command. Paddles in rest position on the gunwale at 90 degrees.

Slow the Boat: Put the blade in the water to slow down the boat.

Stop the Boat: Stop the boat. Stopping requires backward strokes.

Take It Away: Begin paddling.

Watch Your Paddles Left: The boat is approaching an obstruction on the left side.

Watch Your Paddles Right: The boat is approaching an obstruction on the right side.

龙 Additional Readings 船

Books

Clark, Nancy. *Nancy Clark's Sports Nutrition Guidebook*, 4th ed. Champaign, IL: Human Kinetics, 2008.

Crocker, Peter R.E., ed. *Sport Psychology: a Canadian Perspective*. Toronto: Pearson Prentice-Hall, 2007.

Kinakin, Ken. *Optimal Muscle Training*. Windsor, ON: Human Kinetics, 2004.

McDonald, Albert, and Suzanne McKenzie. *Technical Coaching Manual for Dragon Boat Paddling*, 4th ed. Dragon Boat Canada, 2008.

Medley-Marks, Vivian. *Something Completely Different*. Code Pink Books, 2004.

Orlick, Terry. *In Pursuit of Excellence*, 4th ed. Champaign, IL: Human Kinetics, 2008.

Tocher, Michele. *How to Ride a Dragon: Women with Breast Cancer Tell Their Stories*. Toronto: Key Porter Books, 2002.

Ungerleider, Steven. *Mental Training for Peak Performance: Top Athletes Reveal the Mind Exercises They Use to Excel*. Emmaus, PA: Rodale, 2005.

Weider, Ben, and Joe Weider. *The Edge: Ben and Joe Weider's Guide to Ultimate Strength, Speed, and Stamina*. New York: Avery, 2002.

Magazines

Athletic Insight (refereed e-journal on sports psychology). Accessed at *www.athleticinsight.com*.

Dragon Boat World International. Accessed at *www.dragonboatworldinternational.com*.

Nutrition Action Health Letter, Centre for Science in the Public Interest. Accessed at *www.cspinet.org/nah/canada*.

The Sports Journal, United States Sports Academy (e-journal). Accessed at *www.thesportsjournal.org*.

龙 Internet Resources 船

DRAGON BOAT TEAMS, CLUBS, AND ORGANIZATIONS

International Governing Body

International Dragon Boat Federation: *www.idbf.org*.

National Governing Bodies

Dragon Boat Canada: *www.dragonboat.ca*.
United States Dragon Boat Federation: *http://usdbf.com*.

LINKS TO TEAMS/CLUBS

Abreast in a Boat (Breast Cancer Survivor Teams): *www.abreastinaboat.com*.
Dragon Boat Canada: *www.dragonboat.ca*.
Dragon Boat East: *www.dragonboateast.ca*.
Dragon Boat West: *www.dragonboatwest.net*.

Dragon Boat Racing: Organizations, Team Sites, and Pages: *www.boatowners.com/canoe_dragonboats.htm*.

LINKS TO RACES AND REGATTAS

Dragon Boat Canada: *www.dragonboat.ca*.
Dragon Boat East: *www.dragonboateast.ca*.
Dragon Boat West: *www.dragonboatwest.net*.
Dragonboat.net: *www.dragonboat.net*.

DRAGON BOAT FORUMS

Dragon Boat Forum: *http://groups.yahoo.com/group/DragonBoatForum*.
Dragon Boat Rankings/Forum: *www.network54.com/Forum/135730*.
Dragon Boat West Forum: *www.dragonboatwest.net/index.php?action=forum*.

Dragon Boat Rankings
≠ ≠

Dragon Boat Canada: *www.dragonboat.ca*.
Dragon Boat Rankings: *www.geocities.com/dragon_boat_rankings*.

Select Sources for IDBF-Licensed Dragon Boat Manufacturers
≠ ≠

BuK: *www.dragon.de*.
Champion Boats: *www.metroevent.com/dalian*.
Gemini Dragon Boat: *www.gemini.gda.pl*.
IDBF: *www.idbf.org/documents_licensed.php*.
Pel Kayaks: *www.dragonboat.nl*.
Plastex Composite: *www.plastex.home.pl*.

Select Sources for IDBF-Licensed Racing Paddles
≠ ≠

Apex Composites Inc.: *www.apexcomposites.com*.
Burnwater: *www.burnwater.com*.
Chinook Paddles: *www.chinookpaddles.com*.
Grey Owl Paddles: *www.greyowlpaddles.com*.
IDBF: *www.idbf.org/documents_licensed.php*.
Simon River Sports: *www.simonriversports.com*.
Typhoon 8: *www.typhoon8.com*.
ZRE: *www.zre.com*.

Paddle Listings and Ratings

Dragon Boat West, Paddle Ratings: *www.freewebs.com/paddlerating*.
Dragonglobe.com: dragon boat talk for dragon boaters: reviews [of paddles]: *www.dragonglobe.com/?page_id=15*.
IDBF: *www.idbf.org/documents_licensed.php*.
www.freewebs.com/paddlerating/#Burnwater.

SELECT SOURCES FOR ERGOMETERS

≠ ≠

Concept2: *www.concept2.com*.
KayakPro: *www.kayakpro.com*.
Paddle One: *www.paddleone.com*.

SELECT SOURCES FOR DRAGON BOAT TRAINING

≠ ≠

Dragon Boat Training in Norwich, CT, *Steering* (with Matt Smith): *www.22dragons.com*.
Hong Kong Island Paddle Club, *Training Manual*: *www.hkipc.com/training.php*.
Ocean Paddler TV: *www.oceanpaddler.tv*.
Outrigger Performance Advantage: *www.opadvantage. net*.
Stratford Dragon Boat Club, *Training and Preparation Manual*: *www.stratforddragonboat. com/training.htm*.
Stratford Dragon Boat Club, *Weight Training*: *www. stratforddragonboat.com/training.htm*.

SELECT SOURCES FOR NUTRITION AND PERSONAL TRAINING

≠ ≠

Canada's Food Guide: Accessed at *www.hc-sc.gc.ca/ fn-an/food-guide-aliment/index-eng.php*.
Canadian Personal Training Network: *www.cptn.com*.
Canfitpro (a non-profit body that provides training and certification for trainers): *www.canfitpro.com/ default_eng.htm*.
Coaching Association of Canada (includes resources for coaches and athletes): *www.coach.ca*.
Department of Nutrition, Harvard School of Public Health: *www.hsph.harvard.edu/nutritionsource/ index.html*.
Dietitians of Canada (includes a directory of practitioners and information on nutrition): *www. dietitians.ca*.
Exercise database with video instruction: *www.myfit. ca*.
Instruction and demonstration for correct execution of exercises: *www.exrx.net/index.html*.
Instruction and workouts using the Concept2 ergometer: *www.concept2.com/us/training/default. asp*.

CLOTHING (SOME EXAMPLES OF RESOURCES FOR CLOTHING)

JOS Technical Sportswear
Louis Garneau
McNie Protective Paddling Gear
Mountain Equipment Co-Op
Paddles Ready
Pulling Water
Regatta Sport
Row West Clothing
Salus Marine Wear
Simon River Sports
Squidwear
Sugoi
Team Clothing
True North Sportswear
Typhoon Paddling

DRAGON BOATING SERVICE PROVIDERS

Alkame Dragon Boat Services: *www.alkame.ca*.

Dragon Boat East: *www.dragonboateast.ca*.
Great White North: *www.gwndragonboat.com*.
Lively Dragon Dragon Boat Club: *www.dragon-boats.com*.
22Dragons: *www.22dragons.com*.
Water's Edge Sport Performance, Inc.: *www.watersedgesportperformance.com*.

OTHER INTERNET RESOURCES

American and Canadian Dragon Boat Teams, Club Crews, Races, and Festivals: *www.dragonboatnet.com/index.php*.
Beast Blogs (frequent news and views about dragon boat): *http://dragonboateast.ca*.
Breast Cancer Survivors Dragon Boat Racing Around the World: *www.bcsdragonboatraces.com/index.htm*.
Dragon Boat Channel: *www.thedragonboatchannel.com, Dragon-Boats.net*.
Dragonglobe.com (blog website aimed at those interested in dragon boating and dragon boat products and events): *www.dragonglobe.com*.
YouTube: *www.youtube.com*.

龙 Editors and Contributors 船

ARLENE CHAN

Arlene's passion for dragon boating was launched nine years ago when she was researching her third children's book, *Awakening the Dragon: The Dragon Boat Festival*. Her two earlier books are *The Spirit of the Dragon: The Story of Jean Lumb, a Proud Chinese Canadian*, selected as a Choice Book by the Canadian Children's Book Centre, and *The Moon Festival: A Chinese Mid-Autumn Festival*, shortlisted for the Silver Birch Award. When she is not paddling on Lake Ontario, she lives on land in Toronto.

PAM LUMB COLLETT

Pam graduated from York University in physical education and brings extensive experience from regional, provincial, and national high performance sports programs. She is a specialist in the theory and technical components of the National Coaching Certification Program, an internationally ranked official, and a sport consultant. She has been an instructor at Seneca College and University of Toronto's Department of Kinesiology, as well as a consultant with Gymnastics Ontario. She has provided sports commentaries for Rogers Television and CBC Television.

JIM FARINTOSH

ANDREW FOX

Jim has 20 years of experience in the sport of dragon boating as well as decades as a sprint paddler. He has been the Canadian National Team coach for the past 12 years, winning 11 world titles, as well as two open titles at the Hong Kong International Festival. For the past 10 years, he has coached the Mayfair Predators, consistently one of the top premier mixed club crews in Canada, recently winning three gold medals in the 2008 Club Crew World Championships in Penang, Malaysia. Jim is a retired mathematics teacher and is director of the Great White North dragon boat training camps held every April in Florida. Jim is married to Cathy and has two childre

Andrew has been active in dragon boating as a coach and paddler since 1991. He has competed internationally on national crews and on his Toronto team, Mayfair Predators. Among his medals are those from 1999 Hong Kong; 2003 Nations Cup, Poland; 2005 World Championships, Berlin; 2005 North American Championships, Toronto; 2006 World Club Crew Championships, Toronto; 2007 World Championships, Sydney, Australia; and, most recently, 2008 World Club Crew Championships, Penang, Malaysia. For over 10 years, Andrew has been coaching teams that are looking to improve and compete, including the Outer Harbour Dragon Boat Club Premier Women who competed in the last two World Club Crew Championships.

Awesome Guy

Our Coach 2009 + 2010 (bringing here)

MIKE HASLAM

JAMIE HOLLINS, B.KIN, CK, CSCS

Mike is currently the executive president of the International Dragon Boat Federation (IDBF), a position he has held since 1995; the president of the European Dragon Boat Federation; and chair of the British Dragon Boat Racing Association.

Before becoming involved in dragon boat racing, Mike was active in canoe sport as a competitor, coach, and official. He organized both national and international canoe regattas in the United Kingdom and officiated at the world level. Mike was a manager of the British Olympic Canoe Team in 1976 and 1980 and the quartermaster for the whole British Olympic Team in 1984. As the director of the World Canoe Racing Championships in Nottingham, England, his interest in dragon boat started when he organized ad hoc dragon boat races as part of the supporting events for the World Canoe Racing Championships.

After an inspiring trip to Hong Kong in 1985, Mike founded the British Dragon Boat Racing Association and organized the first British National Championships in 1987. The founding of the European Federation followed in 1990 and, in 1991, Mike helped to set up the IDBF and became its first secretary-general. Mike lives in South Wales, near Cardiff.

Jamie is a kinesiology graduate from McMaster University and a Certified Strength and Conditioning Specialist (CSCS) from the National Strength and Conditioning Association (NSCA). He has also worked in the fitness rehabilitation industry as a certified kinesiologist (CK) under the Ontario Kinesiology Association (OKA). Jamie is a flatwater/dragon boat paddler and coach who has provided fitness and conditioning programs for paddlers of all athletic ability, from beginners to national crew members. He is the strength and conditioning director of ATP: Athletic Training Professionals in Pickering, Ontario.

SUSAN HUMPHRIES

KAMINI JAIN

Susan has been an avid dragon boat paddler for the past 10 years. She was an original member of Toronto's Breast Cancer Survivor team, Dragons Abreast, and was hooked on the sport from the moment her paddle first hit the water.

Since 2000, Susan has raced with Premier, Senior, and Grand Dragon crews. She has competed in the European, North American and World Club Crew Championships and has been a member of several Canadian national crews racing in the World Dragon Boat Racing Championships. She was instrumental in the introduction of the Grand Dragon Racing Class at the World Championships.

Susan has also been active in the governance of the sport through her work with Dragon Boat Canada. She served as president of DBC and is now a member of the board of directors. Susan lives in Burlington, Ontario.

Kamini brings physiological knowledge and a highly competitive and diversified canoe-sport background to her dragon boat coaching. A master's degree in comparative physiology from Simon Fraser University provides her with a strong background in exercise physiology. Twenty-four years of pursuing excellence in paddle sports, competing in and coaching sprint kayak, dragon boat, outrigger canoe, marathon canoe, and surf-ski at national and international levels provides her with a comprehensive coaching approach. Ending in 2004, Kamini competed for nine years on the Canadian Sprint Kayak Team during which she earned several World Cup medals and was a finalist at both the 2000 and 2004 Olympic Games. Since retiring from the national crew, Kamini's main paddling focus has been on dragon boat. She coached False Creek Racing Canoe Club men's and mixed teams to repeated Alcan Vancouver International Dragon Boat Festival victories, four 2006 Club Crew Championship victories, and gold and silver medals at the 2005 World Dragon Boat Racing Championships. Kamini is the coach for the Canadian Premier Open and Mixed Crews for the 2009 World Dragon Boat Racing Championships. In 2008, Kamini launched a paddle sport coaching company called Right Angle Performance.

GERRY KAVANAGH

MIKE KERKMANN

After nine years of racing go-carts and Ford Formulas, Gerry founded Apex Composites, based in Burlington, Ontario. Over the years, the company's focus has evolved from racing car body work to the manufacture of aerospace composites.

The paddle division was started when a friend suggested that they develop a carbon-fibre paddle to meet the newly released IDBF specifications. Not long after, they began the development of a durable paddle suitable for fleet use. Apex now produces a range of paddles for both the novice and elite-level paddler.

A self-described "beer-league" paddler, Gerry enjoys the camaraderie and team work of dragon boat.

Mike is the co-founder and current president of Great White North Communications, North America's largest dragon boat equipment and service supplier. Through his company he has been instrumental in the development of a number of festivals in Canada and the United States, including the highly successful GWN Dragon Boat Challenge.

In recognition of his work in promoting safety in dragon boat, Mike, along with Adrian Lee of Vancouver, received a Special Boating Safety Recognition Award at the 2001 Canadian Safe Boating Awards.

Mike's passion for dragon boat extends well beyond a business relationship. His leadership during the early years of Dragon Boat Canada and his role in the development of standards in the design and manufacture of dragon boats have made a significant impact on the growth of the sport in Canada. He is the Pan American representative on the IDBF Council. Mike, who lives in Toronto, is married and has two children.

Dr. David Levy, B.A., MD, CCFP, FCFP, DOHS, Dip. Sport Med.

program, and the co-director of McMaster's Primary Care Sport Medicine Fellowship Program.

Dr. Levy is a graduate of McMaster University where he is an associate clinical professor in the Department of Family Medicine with a cross appointment in the Department of Physical Medicine and Rehabilitation. In his practice, the first primary care sport medicine clinic in southern Ontario established in 1983, he has been looking after athletes of all ages and talent levels for many years.

Dr. Levy has been the team physician to the Hamilton Tiger Cats Football Club for 35 years, the medical director of the Toronto Rock Professional Lacrosse team since its inception, and a physician to McMaster Varsity sports teams for over 29 years. He is also on the medical staff of the Hamilton Bulldogs American Hockey League team and the team physician to Hamilton's breast cancer dragon boat team, Knot A Breast, for the past 10 years.

The former chair of the Ontario Medical Association Section on Sport Medicine and member of the Board of Directors, Canadian Academy of Sport Medicine, Dr. Levy is currently on the board of directors of the Hamilton Sport and Musculoskeletal Physicians Group, the chair of the Program Advisory Committee for the Sheridan College Athletic Therapy

Kathy Levy

Kathy, a registered nurse, opened Hamilton's first sports medicine clinic with her husband, Dr. David Levy, in 1983. Thirteen years later Kathy was diagnosed with breast cancer. Her life took another dramatic turn when she learned about the work of Dr. Don McKenzie and how dragon boating was helping breast cancer survivors like her. Kathy established Knot A Breast, the first breast cancer team in Hamilton and the ninth of its kind in Canada. Now celebrating 11 years, Knot A Breast has grown from 22 to 75 dragon boaters who compete at a world-class level as a crew, winning the 2005 North American Club Crew Breast Cancer Championships, or as individuals on other teams competing in Berlin.

ALBERT McDONALD

SUZANNE McKENZIE

Albert is a national level coach from Dartmouth, Nova Scotia, with 16 medals (six gold) in international dragon boat competition in the Premier and Senior divisions. He has competed as an elite flatwater sprint canoer and paddler for 40 years and coached for almost 30. Currently, he is the head coach and general manager of Dragon Boat East, a service provider for dragon boat festivals across North America.

OUR
COACH
2008

Suzanne, who has over 20 years of paddling experience, has been a medallist in national women's C4 and war canoe. She is a member of the Dragon Boat East club crew that won the 2008 Quebec Cup and secured the national title in the Premier Open Division at the 2008 National Championships. She was also on the Premier Women's National Crew that won four gold medals at the 2007 World Championships in Sydney, Australia. Suzanne is a full-time teacher and the co-author of the level one coaching manual for Dragon Boat Canada. She lives in Halifax, Nova Scotia.

ELEANOR NIELSEN, REG. N., M.H.SC.

MATT ROBERT

Eleanor retired from the national office of the Canadian Cancer Society where she was director of programs from 1991 to 2001. She was responsible for program development, implementation, and evaluation of Public Education and Patient Services programs across Canada. In this position she participated in many breast cancer organizations and met members of the first breast cancer dragon boat team, Abreast In A Boat, in 1996. Impressed by their energy and enthusiasm for dragon boating, she co-founded the Toronto team, Dragons Abreast, in 1997. Since then, she has been an active paddler. She is a member of the Steering Committee of the International Breast Cancer Paddlers Commission and co-chair of the Ontario Breast Cancer Dragon Boat Network. Eleanor spends her non-paddling time volunteering for a number of cancer organizations, gardening, and enjoying time with her husband, Charles, and their six grandchildren.

Matt has an extensive background in paddling. A former Quebec provincial team sprint paddler and member of several National Premier dragon boat crews, he was integral to the building of the successful Wong's Dragon Boat Club and coached the Montreal Women's Team that won gold at the 2006 Club Crew World Championships in Rome, and most recently, in Penang, Malaysia, 2008.

In 2003, he co-founded, with fellow paddler, Matt Smith, 22Dragons where he is currently the head coach. Matt is regarded as one of the top dragon boat coaches in Canada and is known for his skill in steering boats down the racecourse.

A former director of Dragon Boat Canada, Matt was the first chair of the Technical Committee and was instrumental in the development of Dragon Boat Canada coaching certification. He lives in Montreal.

MATT SMITH

Matt has been coaching dragon boat teams since 1996 and has more than 20 years of paddling experience. He is president of Dragon Boat Canada and a former national crew dragon boater. After graduating with a degree in electrical engineering and working for two years in the field, Matt subsequently co-founded the 22Dragons dragon boat training centre in 2003 with Matt Robert. Matt coaches several crews at 22Dragons, including the premier mixed crew Verdun Adrenaline, which placed fourth at the 2008 CCWC in Penang, Malaysia, and the Montreal Dragon Boat Club Premier Women, who swept their division, winning three gold medals (200, 500, and 2,000 metres) at the 2006 Club Crew World Championships in Toronto, and followed up with a repeat sweep of gold medal wins at the 2008 World Championships in Penang, Malaysia. He lives in Montreal.